S. Hrg. 113–438

INDIAN LAW AND ORDER COMMISSION REPORT: A ROADMAP FOR MAKING NATIVE AMERICA SAFER

HEARING

BEFORE THE

COMMITTEE ON INDIAN AFFAIRS
UNITED STATES SENATE

ONE HUNDRED THIRTEENTH CONGRESS

SECOND SESSION

FEBRUARY 12, 2014

Printed for the use of the Committee on Indian Affairs

U.S. GOVERNMENT PRINTING OFFICE

WASHINGTON : 2014

90–933 PDF

For sale by the Superintendent of Documents, U.S. Government Printing Office
Internet: bookstore.gpo.gov   Phone: toll free (866) 512–1800; DC area (202) 512–1800
Fax: (202) 512–2104   Mail: Stop IDCC, Washington, DC 20402–0001

CONTENTS

Page

Hearing held on February 12, 2014 1
Statement of Senator Barrasso 2
Statement of Senator Begich 3
Statement of Senator Cantwell 1
Statement of Senator Heitkamp 3
Statement of Senator Murkowski 16
    Prepared statement 18
Statement of Senator Tester 25

WITNESSES

Eid, Troy A., Chairman, Indian Law and Order Commission 29
    Joint prepared statement 31
Ellis, Affie, Commissioner, Indian Law and Order Commission 27
Jerue, Tami Truett, Director of Social Services/Tribal Administrator, Anvik
    Tribal Council 37
    Prepared statement 39
Purdon, Hon. Timothy Q., U.S. Attorney, District of North Dakota, U.S.
    Department of Justice 8
    Prepared statement 9
Washburn, Hon. Kevin, Assistant Secretary—Indian Affairs, U.S. Department
    of the Interior 4
    Prepared statement 6

APPENDIX

Great Plains Tribal Chairman's Association, prepared statement 56
Posey, Ivan D., Chairman, Montana-Wyoming Tribal Leaders Council, pre-
    pared statement 55
Response to written questions submitted to Troy A. Eid and Affie Ellis by:
    Hon. Mark Begich 68
    Hon. Tim Johnson 67
Response to written questions submitted to Hon. Timothy Q. Purdon by:
    Mark Begich 80
    Hon. Heidi Heitkamp 71
    Hon. Tim Johnson 78
Willman, Elaine D., Director, Community Development and Tribal Affairs,
    Village of Hobart, prepared statement 65
Written questions submitted to Hon. Kevin Washburn 81

INDIAN LAW AND ORDER COMMISSION REPORT: A ROADMAP FOR MAKING NATIVE AMERICA SAFER

WEDNESDAY, FEBRUARY 12, 2014

U.S. SENATE,
COMMITTEE ON INDIAN AFFAIRS,
Washington, DC.

The Committee met, pursuant to notice, at 3:47 p.m. in room 628, Dirksen Senate Office Building, Hon. Maria Cantwell, Chairman of the Committee, presiding.

OPENING STATEMENT OF HON. MARIA CANTWELL, U.S. SENATOR FROM WASHINGTON

The CHAIRWOMAN. The Senate Committee on Indian Affairs will come to order.

Today we are having an oversight hearing on the Indian Law and Order Commission Report: A Roadmap for Making Native America Safer. I apologize to everyone, we thought we were going to have this hearing at 2:30 and obviously votes got in the way. I know everyone is worried about impending weather, so we appreciate your patience.

We are going to hear from two people today, the Assistant Secretary, thank you for being here again, Assistant Secretary Washburn, and the Honorable Timothy Purdon, who is U.S. Attorney, District of North Dakota, U.S. Department of Justice.

Obviously this Committee is soon going to be chaired by my colleague, Jon Tester, so under his leadership I know we will continue to guide and shape Federal law to strengthen the government-to-government relationship between tribes, and the people who live in Indian Country and also the Alaska Native people. So I look very much forward to working with Senator Tester, and as a member of this Committee I plan to continue to be active.

Today's hearing is on the Indian Law and Order Commission Report: A Roadmap for Making Native America Safer. We will hear from the Committee's work to improve public safety and justice in Indian Country. The report was mandated under the Tribal Law and Order Act of 2010, which was enacted while a former colleague, Senator Dorgan, was Chair of the Committee. And the report specifically identifies problems that exist with public safety and justice in Indian Country and Alaska Native villages. More importantly, it proposes recommendations to address some of these issues.

(1)

Some of the Commission's recommendations require legislative action. I look forward to working with my colleagues to tackle some of those barriers that exist to reducing crime in Indian Country. I would also recognize the amazing work that tribes are already doing to reduce crime and making their communities safer. I want to acknowledge the tribes in my home State of Washington who are making improvements in public safety. Tribes in Washington are operating tribal courts that are finding new, innovative ways to address recidivism, including being some of the first tribes to provide defense counsel to indigent defendants. I am also proud that the Puyallup Tribe is one of the first three tribes to selected as part of a pilot project to exercise tribal jurisdiction over domestic violence crimes on the reservations. This pilot project was established under VAWA reauthorization last year, when we fought so hard to strengthen the tribal provisions in that. And this pilot project will allow a few tribes on an accelerated basis to begin exercising tribal jurisdiction over certain domestic violence crimes on reservations, specifically domestic violence crimes committed by non-tribal members.

While VAWA was a step forward for all of the tribes in Indian Country, there is still a lot more work to be done to bring in parity and to make tribal jurisdictions more responsible for the tribes within their land base. As we all know, the patchwork of jurisdiction in Indian Country creates severe problems for law enforcement and judicial systems to make arrests and prosecute crimes. And these jurisdictional problems are only exacerbated by the remoteness of some of our tribal areas.

So as the Commission report illustrates, nowhere is this problem more challenging than in Alaska. I know my colleague Senator Begich is here, and Senator Murkowski and I had a chance to talk about this last August when I was visiting Alaska. Alaska's 229 federally-recognized tribes have no land base and many villages are virtually where there is no law enforcement presence.

So this issue is vital. The Commission has dedicated so much time in the report to what has happened in Alaska Native villages. So I am so glad my colleague Senator Begich is here this afternoon. I continue to say that we will work with him and other members of this Committee on this important issue.

Now I would like to turn it over to my colleague, the Vice Chairman of the Committee.

STATEMENT OF HON. JOHN BARRASSO, U.S. SENATOR FROM WYOMING

Senator BARRASSO. Thank you very much, Madam Chairwoman, for holding this important hearing. Public safety in Native American communities is a complex and serious issue. It has been a top priority for the tribes in Wyoming, the Eastern Shoshone and the Northern Arapaho Tribes, for a long time.

Back in the 111th Congress, I co-sponsored a bill that became the Tribal Law and Order Act. This Act was intended to address certain deficiencies in the Indian Country criminal justice system. It established the Indian Law and Order Commission to study and make recommendations to further improve the system. Today we are going to hear the Commission's findings and recommendations.

More importantly, we are going to hear from Federal and tribal officials on where we should go from here.

I want to express my appreciation to Affie Ellis, who is here with us today and will be testifying on the second panel, and Ivan Posey, who has also been involved, for considerable contributions to the Commission's work. Affie served as the Commissioner and traveled to some of the most remote locations in this Country to hear from Indian people. Ivan Posey was scheduled to testify today, but he experienced flight delays. He served on the Commission's tribal advisory committee.

So thank you to both of my fellow Wyoming citizens and the Commission for all their hard work on this report. I look forward to the testimony today. I thank you very much, Madam Chairwoman.

The CHAIRWOMAN. Would either of my colleagues like to make an opening statement? Senator Begich or Senator Heitkamp?

STATEMENT OF HON. MARK BEGICH,
U.S. SENATOR FROM ALASKA

Senator BEGICH. Madam Chair, I will be brief, because I know we have some great witnesses. But I thank you for holding this hearing. I know we made a request and I appreciate your honoring that request and having this hearing today, especially because one of the sections is dedicated to Alaska. Sometimes we like things dedicated to Alaska, this is not necessarily something we like to have dedicated to Alaska.

But I think it is very important, because the points that it brings out are things that we can do, and the problems we have in Alaska. So I thank you for that. And I know I will have some questions, especially around a piece of legislation I had sponsored on the Safe Villages and Families Act, and how we can move forward to create a better environment for rural Alaska, which is diverse and broad and has some incredible issues, as your report shows.

So thank you, Madam Chair, and I would say again, your leadership here has been exceptional. I will miss you as chair, but I know you are going to the Small Business Committee, which is also a very important committee, not only for this Country, but I will tell you, for Alaska in many ways. Thank you for our service here. I look forward to the questions.

The CHAIRWOMAN. Thank you. Senator Heitkamp?

STATEMENT OF HON. HEIDI HEITKAMP,
U.S. SENATOR FROM NORTH DAKOTA

Senator HEITKAMP. Thank you, and thank you to both you and to Vice Chairman Barrasso for holding this hearing. And I want to thank you, Chairwoman, for the excellent work. I am thrilled to find out that you are going to remain on the Committee. I know we have many, many issues to look forward to a cooperative venture on.

As a former Attorney General from North Dakota, I have seen first hand the law and order challenges of the give tribes in our State. Our tribes are known as large land-based tribes. For example, Standing Rock Sioux Reservation is approximately 36 square miles, or 2.3 million acres. It is roughly the size of Connecticut.

And for that entire land mass, the tribe has only 24 law enforcement officers. This is considered relatively well-staffed, compared to many places.

The high rates of violence, substance abuse and incarceration affect everyone, whether or not they are tribal members. You can simply not live with these conditions near you and not see the toll that they take on the social fabric of our community and certainly of the tribes.

I don't think we should be proud to live in a country where 34 percent of Native American women will be raped in their lifetime. I don't think we should be proud to live in a country where almost 40 percent of Indian people will be subjected to domestic violence. Violent crime rates across Indian Country are twice as high as the national average, and Indian children experience abuse at rates 50 percent higher than their non-Native counterparts.

I look forward to looking for solutions, not just studies, but actually having a broad conversation about how we can in fact begin to change the trajectory. In fact, I think generationally, we have to do this if we are going to continue to have healthy communities in Indian Country. There should be no solution off the table, which is why the Violence Against Women Act, which for the first time began to talk about working cooperatively with tribal courts is so significant. It was a leap, it was hard-fought. But yet it is one step, I think, in the right direction to getting justice for Indian people, both in Indian Country and off Indian Country.

So I want to thank you, Madam Chairwoman, but I also need to say hello to Tim, because Tim Purdon and I have worked together on issues throughout North Dakota for a lot of years. He has made this issue definitely his prime focus as U.S. Attorney. I appreciate that focus, Tim. Thank you.

The CHAIRWOMAN. Again, thank you to the witnesses, and we are sorry for the delay. Thank you for your patience, and we look forward to your testimony. We will start with you, Assistant Secretary Washburn. Thank you for being here.

STATEMENT OF HON. KEVIN WASHBURN, ASSISTANT SECRETARY—INDIAN AFFAIRS, U.S. DEPARTMENT OF THE INTERIOR

Mr. WASHBURN. Madam Chair, thank you for scheduling this hearing. Thank you for your long leadership. We are grateful for that and glad that you are going to be continuing your service on the Committee.

Mr. Vice Chair, thank you for our service too, and your support of TLOA and committee members, you have both been very active members of that committee. It is always an honor to appear before you. Thank you.

I want to first thank the Department of Justice for the great partnership we have developed. I have to say, this Department of Justice has really made a lot of progress in the last five years and really, really brought justice in Indian Country forward a long way. With the support of this Committee, with TLOA and the VAWA reauthorization, we have really made some major accomplishments for self-determination for Indian Country. After TLOA and after VAWA, though, we still have a ways to go. I am really grateful to

Chairman Eid and the rest of the Commission for keeping the conversation going, because we haven't solved all the problems. We have many more to solve, and the conversation now continues.

As an academic, I had the great honor to appear before the Commission, thanks to the invitation of Chairman Eid. I am very supportive of its work.

There are a lot of very specific recommendations in the report. Frankly, that is very, very helpful, because it really helps to have someone that has really looked carefully, thought through the difficult details, read the scholarship and talked to people and held hearings and really made some specific recommendations.

We have not consulted with tribes specifically on any of those recommendations, though, so one of the things I thought I might do in my testimony is talk about some overarching principles that I think come through in the report and that are very important principles that we can agree on.

One of those, first, is that tribal law enforcement officers need to be equal partners in Indian Country. They need access to all the information that regular police officers outside of Indian Country have, criminal police reports and that sort of thing. They need to have the information available to do their job. They need access to all the information that is necessary to accomplish public safety.

A second compelling theme in the report that we strongly agree on is that all tribes have an interest in public safety. This includes tribes in Public Law 280 States, like Alaska. That is an important principle and we are troubled by the information that the Commission has helped to shed light on in Alaska. I thank Senator Begich for his leadership in trying to address that. It is a real problem, and we need to have all issues on the table to figure out how to address them. They aren't easy to address because there are some fiscal challenges there. But we need to be talking about them.

A third compelling theme in the report I think is that where the United States has invested strategically in Indian Country with its financial resources, we have seen great success. We have a lot of examples of that, including at the Wind River Reservation. And we can't be blind to that. We have invested millions of dollars in increasing money in this area during the Obama Administration, and it has really made a difference. The Justice Department has invested hundreds of millions of dollars in grant programs. That money has really accomplished a lot. It hasn't solved all the problems, but it has really moved things forward tremendously.

Another compelling theme in the report, and in the interest of time, the last one I will talk about, is that public safety is more than just law enforcement. It includes a lot of other issues. And providing public safety requires is to address issues like substance abuse and re-entry and other issues aside from just addressing individual crimes. In addition to the Justice Department, we have many other important partners in this area, too, including IHS and SAMHSA and other entities across the Federal Government. There is a dramatic coordination challenge that we must address so that we are providing good services to all the people in Indian Country and meeting the needs of victims, defendants and those children who are exposed to violence and other people who are exposed to these crimes.

So I will stop there, because I had far more rather be talking about the things that you have an interest in thank taking up all of my time. I am grateful to you for holding this hearing and I look forward to your questions. Thank you.

[The prepared statement of Mr. Washburn follows:]

PREPARED STATEMENT OF HON. KEVIN WASHBURN, ASSISTANT SECRETARY—INDIAN AFFAIRS, U.S. DEPARTMENT OF THE INTERIOR

Good afternoon Chairwoman Cantwell, Vice Chairman Barrasso, and members of the Committee. Thank you for inviting the Department of the Interior (Department) to provide testimony on the Indian Law and Order Commission Report: "A Roadmap for Making Native America Safer." I am pleased to be here.

The Administration continues to prioritize the issue of addressing public safety in Tribal communities. This priority is shared by Secretary Sally Jewell, myself, Tribal leaders and members of this Committee. The Administration strongly supported enactment of the Tribal Law and Order Act, which created the Indian Law and Order Commission (Commission). The Act required the Commission to conduct a comprehensive study of law enforcement and criminal justice in tribal communities, develop recommendations for modifications and improvements to justice systems at the Tribal, federal, and state levels, and submit to the President and Congress a report that contains a detailed statement of the findings and conclusions of the Commission. The Indian Law and Order Commission Report: "A Roadmap for Making Native America Safer," (Report) was delivered to the President in November 2013.

Most of the Department's work in this area is carried out by the Bureau of Indian Affairs-Office of Justice Services, led by Director Darren Cruzan. In reviewing the Report, the Department saw much more than specific recommendations. The Report included overarching principles that can help strengthen justice and public safety in Indian country. We find several broad principles or themes within the Report that are crucial to improving public safety in Indian country. The Department has prioritized public safety in Indian Country in its appropriation requests in recent years.

The first is that Tribal law enforcement officers should be equal partners of the public safety community. The Report touched on the importance of increasing access to public safety information that is collected and used by all federal, Tribal and state public safety entities. It is essential that the Department provide Tribes with full and immediate access to criminal justice-related information related to their communities. Tribes must have appropriate information necessary to exercise their inherent criminal jurisdiction effectively under Tribal law as provided by the Tribal Law and Order Act of 2010 (TLOA) and the Violence Against Women Act Reauthorization Amendments of 2013 (VAWA). The Department has drafted a formal protocol to be used by all direct service BIA duty stations for this purpose.

The Department is committed to not only sharing and providing access to information, but also working in partnership with Tribal public safety agencies to strengthen public safety in Indian Country through intergovernmental cooperation. This intergovernmental cooperation includes entering into Deputation Agreements with the Tribes which enables officers working for Tribal police departments with established Deputation Agreements to apply for Special Law Enforcement Commissions (SLEC's). Special Law Enforcement Commissions allow Tribal police officers to enforce certain federal laws in Indian Country. Tribal police officers who put their lives on the line just like federal, state, county and municipal police officers deserve the same level access to information that those officers have.

We consistently cooperate and dialogue with our public safety partners. These collaborations include our federal, Tribal and state partners in public safety. As sister federal agencies, we must collaborate and communicate with each other on public safety issues in Indian Country. Pursuant to our government-to-government relationship with the Tribal Nations, we must consult with Tribal Nations in addressing the public safety concerns in Indian Country. Moreover, since each Tribe is located within a state, and sometimes two or more states, it is paramount that we facilitate collaboration and communication between Tribes and states in addressing public safety concerns in Indian Country.

A second compelling theme of the Report is that all tribes have an interest in public safety. The Report notes that all Tribes have an interest in protecting their members and lands and further recommends that federal funding for Tribal Justice Systems should be made available on equal terms to all federally recognized Tribes, whether their lands are under federal jurisdiction or congressionally authorized state jurisdiction and whether they opt out of federal or state jurisdiction. This Administration strongly supports the principles of Tribal self-determination and self-governance, and we are reviewing the Report and its recommendations to consider if there are ways that we could improve and support the tools available to address their public safety concerns.

In light of the importance of providing public safety to all Indian communities, the Department shares the Department of Justice's views regarding the repeal of Section 910 of VAWA 2013 to allow Alaskan Tribes full civil jurisdiction to issue and enforce domestic violence protection orders to protect Alaska Native victims of domestic violence. This is a sound initial step toward addressing public safety issues for Alaska Natives.

A third compelling theme in the Report is the recognition that where we have strategically invested resources in public safety in Indian Country, we have seen success. Reducing crime in Indian Country is of paramount importance and the Department has been successful in promoting safe communities. In 2010–2011, the Department initiated the Safe Indian Communities—High Priority Performance Goal (HPPG) initiative, which was targeted at achieving a significant reduction in violent criminal offenses of at least 5 percent within 24 months on four Indian reservations by increasing staffing levels to the national rural policing level (2.8 police officers per 1000 residents), implementing a comprehensive strategy involving community policing, tactical deployment, and critical interagency and intergovernmental partnerships. At the end of the measurement period, there was an average 35 percent decrease in violent crime across all four HPPG sites. This result suggests that public safety improvements can be achieved when a comprehensive strategy is implemented.

We also find a compelling theme in the Report that public safety is more than simply law enforcement. The Report recommends a more inclusive view of public safety in Indian Country. This view of public safety includes not just our police officers, but also our detention programs, our Tribal courts programs, and our Indian Services programs, such as Social Services. The Report encourages Tribes to develop and enhance drug courts, wellness courts, residential treatment programs, combined substance abuse treatment-mental health care programs, veterans' courts, clean and sober housing facilities and reentry programs. We need to work harder to address substance abuse and re-entry issues, and facilitating housing and education, and supporting families to improve public safety in Indian Country.

The Department is pursuing an Indian Affairs Agency Priority Goal to reduce recidivism across three targeted reservations by a total of 6 percent. This reduction we hope will be realized through implementing a comprehensive strategy involving alternative courts, increased treatment opportunities, probation programs, and critical interagency and intergovernmental partnerships between Tribal, federal and state stakeholders.

The Department is pleased with the efforts of Tribes and the Department of Justice to address violence against women in Indian Country. The Department has been a partner in these efforts. During the past year, the Department has trained over 300 tribal court personnel on trial court advocacy skills with specific emphasis on issues affecting the safety of Native Women. Specifically, the trainings focused on issues surrounding domestic violence and sexual assault on adults and children. These trainings have been a collaborative effort between, the Department of the Interior, the Department of Justice Access to Justice Office and the United States Attorneys' Offices. Together, we have offered a trial court advocacy training specifically for Tribal court personnel. In an effort to provide realistic and pertinent issues specific to Tribal courts, the trial court advocacy training sessions have included fact patterns which address violence against Native women such as homicide, rape, assault and battery in the home, and workplace.

Conclusion

Thank you for the opportunity to provide the Department's views on the Indian Law and Order Commission Report. The Department is anxious to hear the views of Indian Tribes about all the important subjects addressed in the Report. The Department will continue to work closely with this Committee, Tribal leaders through consultation, and our federal and state partners, collaboratively and cooperatively, to address the law enforcement, corrections and inter-agency issues to better address public safety in Indian Country.

Thank you for focusing attention on the Commission's work. I am available to answer any questions the Committee may have.

The CHAIRWOMAN. Thank you.

Mr. Purdon, thank you very much for being here.

STATEMENT OF HON. TIMOTHY Q. PURDON, U.S. ATTORNEY, DISTRICT OF NORTH DAKOTA, U.S. DEPARTMENT OF JUSTICE

Mr. PURDON. Chairwoman Cantwell and Vice Chair Barrasso, members of the Committee, thank you for inviting me here today. Thank you for the opportunity to provide the perspective of the Department of Justice on the Indian Law and Order Commission's thorough and thoughtful report, A Roadmap for Making Native America Safer, and to discuss the Department's ongoing efforts to ensure public safety in Indian Country.

The Department shares the commitment of this Committee and of the Indian Law and Order Commission to this important issue. We congratulate Chairman Eid and the Commission on the hard work that has culminated in its final report and recommendations. Like the Commission, we at the Department have long been concerned about the high rate of crimes occurring in Indian Country, in particular violence against women and Native children. That is why early in this Administration Attorney General Eric Holder launched a Department-wide initiative to improve public safety in Indian Country.

Since 2009, the Department has engaged in focused and energetic efforts alongside our tribal law enforcement partners to help stem the tide of crime in Indian Country. As the United States Attorney for the District of North Dakota and as the chair of Attorney General Holder's Native American Issues Subcommittee, I am honored to appear before you to discuss this work by the Department to improve public safety in Indian Country. Under Attorney General Holder, the Department has made fighting crime in Indian Country a top priority and has pursued an aggressive strategy, consisting of law enforcement action, but also prosecution, grant funding, training, technical support and most importantly, collaboration with our tribal partners. It is already beginning to show some signs of success.

The Department's renewed focus nationwide on leveraging our partnership with tribal, State, local and Federal law enforcement partners to address violent crime has led to concrete results. Specifically, in just the last four years, U.S. Attorneys offices like mine with responsibility for Indian Country across the Country have seen a number of prosecutions for crimes committed in tribal lands increase by more than 54 percent. This increase was reported to Congress in our Indian Country Investigation and Prosecution Report for calendar years 2011 and 2012 and was presented to Congress last spring.

Specifically, Indian Country caseloads nationwide have increased overall from approximately 1,100 cases filed in fiscal year 2009 to over 1,600 criminal cases filed in fiscal year 2012. This increase in prosecution is due to many factors. But efforts by U.S. Attorneys across the Country to enhance investigative and prosecutorial coordination with tribal partners has been critical to this improvement.

One of the important tools contributing to this improved collaboration is the Department's enhanced Tribal Special Assistant United States Attorney, or SAUSA program. Tribal SAUSAs are recommended and encouraged under the ILOC Commission's report, and I agree that that is a good thing. It is a good program.

SAUSAs are able to are our tribal prosecutors who are cross-deputized and then able to prosecute crimes both in tribal court but also in Federal court as appropriate. These tribal SAUSAs serve to strengthen a tribal government's ability to fight crime, and they also increased the coordination and collaboration between a U.S. Attorney's office and a tribal prosecutor's office.

Since its inception, this program has blossomed with dozens of tribal SAUSAs serving in districts across the Country. We have had a very successful SAUSA program in North Dakota with the Standing Rock tribal prosecutor's office. One of our former SAUSAs is here in the room, he has moved to D.C. and gone to work for the Indian Gaming Commission. Miles Janssen was one of our SAUSAs, prosecuting cases in both tribal court and Federal court, shoulder to shoulder with my AUSAs.

The Department recognizes that the unique challenges to public safety in Indian Country created by jurisdictional schemes, varied jurisdictional schemes and geographic isolation pose unique challenges. It is against this backdrop that the roadmap presents a broad array of recommendations in issue areas as diverse as criminal jurisdiction and juvenile justice. At the Department, we are carefully studying the recommendations and will be reaching out to stakeholders and Federal law enforcement and obviously with our tribal partners to see additional input on solutions that can help address the difficult public safety issues we confront. Meanwhile, we will continue to use our existing authorities to meet our responsibilities and to strengthen capacity at every level of the criminal justice system.

Again, thank you for having me here today, Chairwoman Cantwell. I look forward to answering any questions the Committee may have today.

[The prepared statement of Mr. Purdon follows:]

PREPARED STATEMENT OF HON. TIMOTHY Q. PURDON, U.S. ATTORNEY, DISTRICT OF NORTH DAKOTA, U.S. DEPARTMENT OF JUSTICE

Chairwoman Cantwell, Vice-Chair Barrasso, and Members of the Committee:

Thank you for the opportunity to provide the perspective of the Department of Justice on the Indian Law and Order Commission's thorough, thoughtful, and incisive report, *A Roadmap for Making Native America Safer*, and to discuss the Department's ongoing efforts to ensure public safety in Indian Country. The Department shares the commitment of this Committee and the Indian Law and Order Commission to this important issue, and we congratulate the Commission on the hard work that has culminated in its final report and recommendations. Like the Commission, we at the Department have long been concerned about the high rate of crimes occurring in Indian Country, in particular violence against women. That's why, early in this Administration, Attorney General Eric Holder launched a Department-wide initiative to improve public safety in Indian country. Since 2009, the Department has been engaged in focused and energetic efforts alongside our tribal law enforcement partners to help stem this tide.

As the United States Attorney for the District of North Dakota and Chair of the Attorney General's Native American Issues Subcommittee, I am honored to appear before you to discuss the work of the Department to improve public safety in Indian Country. Since 2009, the Department has made fighting crime in Indian Country a top priority and has pursued an aggressive strategy consisting of law enforcement action, prosecution, grant funding, training, technical support, and collaboration with tribal partners that is already showing success. For example, the Department's renewed commitment to the vigorous prosecution of federal crimes in Indian Country has increased the number of Indian Country prosecutions by United States Attorney's Offices nationwide by more than fifty percent over the past four years.

Nonetheless, the Department recognizes that an increase in federal arrests and prosecutions alone cannot solve all the public safety challenges on the reservations. Accordingly, we have augmented our enhanced focus on law enforcement and prosecutions with additional support for tribal criminal justice institutions. In 2010, the Department answered a call from tribal leaders for a more streamlined, holistic approach to its tribal-specific grant programs by establishing the Coordinated Tribal Assistance Solicitation (CTAS). CTAS helps tribes secure critical federal assistance on a wide array of criminal justice issues, including preventing violence against women, protecting at-risk children, improving community policing, and exploring alternatives to incarceration. Through CTAS, we have awarded nearly $440 million in federal grants to tribes in the past four years. These funds work to directly strengthen the criminal justice system in Indian Country, creating opportunities for increased collaboration with our tribal partners and increased tribal self-determination.

The Department recognizes the unique challenges to public safety in Indian Country created by varied jurisdictional schemes and varying tribal cultures. It is against this backdrop that the *Roadmap* presents a broad array of recommendations in issue areas as diverse as criminal jurisdiction and juvenile justice. We are carefully studying the recommendations and will be reaching out to stakeholders to seek additional input on solutions that can address the difficult public safety issues confronting tribal communities. Meanwhile, we will continue to use our existing authorities to meet our responsibilities and to strengthen capacity at every level of the criminal justice system.

Establishing Unprecedented Levels of Cooperation

Since taking Office, Attorney General Holder has consistently emphasized that combatting violent crime in Indian Country and fostering safe communities is a top priority of the Department of Justice. Attorney General Holder has stated that when it comes to this challenge, we must "recommit ourselves to collaboration on an unprecedented scale." To this end, the Department took steps in early 2010 to ensure that each United States Attorney's Office with responsibilities in Indian Country implemented a district-specific operational plan to formalize its strategy for consulting and working with tribal, state, and local law enforcement, prosecutors, and other leaders, to improve public safety in Indian Country. For example, in North Dakota, our operational plan took the form of an Anti-Violence Strategy that combines enhanced enforcement of federal criminal laws with support for viable crime prevention programs and efforts to build a sustainable offender reentry program. Our plan has now been in place for almost three years and has resulted in unprecedented levels of communication and collaboration between the U.S. Attorney's Office and the tribes in North Dakota as well as a large increase in the number of Indian Country cases being prosecuted by our Office.

The Department's renewed focus nationwide on leveraging partnerships with tribal, local, state, and federal partners to address violent crime has led to concrete results, not just in North Dakota, but across the rest of the country. In just the last four years, U.S. Attorneys' offices with responsibility for Indian Country have seen the number of prosecutions for crimes committed on tribal lands increase by more than 54 percent. This increase was reported to Congress in our *Indian Country Investigation and Prosecution Report* (ICIP) for calendar years (CYs) 2011 and 2012.[1] Specifically, Indian Country caseloads nationwide have increased overall:

- 1,091 criminal cases filed in fiscal year (FY) 2009;
- 1,138 criminal cases filed in FY 2010;
- 1,547 criminal cases filed in FY 2011; and
- 1,677 criminal cases filed in FY 2012.

This increase in prosecutions is due to many factors, but efforts by U.S. Attorneys to enhance investigative and prosecutorial coordination with tribal partners have been critical to this improvement.

A great example of how collaboration improves law enforcement can be found in Montana. In 2010, Montana United States Attorney Mike Cotter began convening bi-monthly meetings involving the federal prosecutors assigned to each reservation, the tribal prosecutors for the reservation, and tribal and federal law enforcement officers. During these meetings, cases arising on a particular reservation during the preceding two-week period are discussed and a decision is reached collaboratively

---

[1] *www.justice.gov/tribal/tloa-report-cy-2011–2012.pdf.*

concerning which jurisdiction—Federal or tribal or both—will prosecute a particular case. This close communication ensures that serious Indian Country crimes are appropriately investigated and that the decision whether a matter will be charged in federal court or tribal court is an informed one.

An important tool contributing to improved collaboration is the Department's enhanced Tribal Special Assistant U.S. Attorney (SAUSA) program. Tribal SAUSAs are tribal prosecutors who are "cross-deputized" and able to prosecute crimes in both tribal court and federal court as appropriate. These Tribal SAUSAs serve to strengthen a tribal government's ability to fight crime and to increase the USAO's coordination with tribal law enforcement personnel. Since its inception, the program blossomed, with dozens of Tribal SAUSAs serving in districts across the country.

To increase the use of Tribal SAUSAs in cases involving violence against Native women, in 2012, the Office on Violence Against Women (OVW) initiated its Violence Against Women Tribal SAUSA Pilot Project, making awards to four tribes in Nebraska, New Mexico, Montana, North Dakota and South Dakota to fund cross-designated tribal prosecutors. The goal of the Tribal SAUSA Pilot Project is that every viable crime of domestic violence, dating violence, sexual assault, and stalking will be prosecuted in federal court, tribal court, or both. We have an OVW-funded SAUSA working in my Office and for the Standing Rock Sioux Tribal Prosecutor. She has tried domestic violence cases in tribal court and has secured prison time in domestic violence cases in federal court as well.

The work of Tribal SAUSAs can also help to accelerate a tribal criminal justice system's implementation of the Tribal Law and Order Act of 2010 and the Violence Against Women Reauthorization Act of 2013. The use of Tribal SAUSAs is expanding and, consistent with the *Roadmap's* Recommendations 3.3 and 3.4, the Department supports strengthening the work of Tribal SAUSAs by improving access to law enforcement sensitive information and witnesses where such access does not exist already.

The SAUSA program is one area that the *Roadmap* acknowledges has the potential to address the broader need for skilled, committed prosecutors working on the ground in Indian Country. To help meet this demand, Attorney General Holder announced last November the Attorney General's Indian Country Fellowship. This fellowship, which will be part of the Attorney General's Honors Program, will inspire and train the next generation of prosecutors to serve in Indian Country. It will create an opportunity for highly qualified law-school graduates to spend three years—primarily in U.S. Attorneys' Offices—working on Indian Country cases and thereby creating a pool of attorneys with deep experience in Federal Indian law, tribal law, and Indian country issues.

The commitment of the U.S. Attorney's Offices in Indian Country has been supported by Department components that have provided much-needed training to law enforcement and prosecutors who are working in Indian Country. For example:

- *National Indian Country Training Initiative (NICTI).* Prosecutors working in Indian Country need specialized training. The NICTI has answered that call. Launched in 2010, it works to ensure that AUSAs and Tribal SAUSAs, as well as state and tribal criminal justice personnel, receive the training and support needed to address the particular challenges relevant to Indian Country prosecutions. For example, in January 2013, the NICTI partnered with the National Strangulation Training Institute to deliver the first-ever national Indian Country training on the investigation and prosecution of non-fatal strangulation and suffocation offenses. The training, held at the National Advocacy Center in Columbia, South Carolina, drew attendance from 17 tribes, U.S. Attorney's Offices, the FBI, and the Bureau of Indian Affairs and provided an in-depth examination of the mechanics of strangulation and suffocation from a medical, legal, and law enforcement perspective.

- *Access to Justice (ATJ).* Since 2011, ATJ has partnered with the U.S. Department of the Interior's Bureau of Indian Affairs, Office of Justice Services, to host a series of tribal court trainings known as the Tribal Court Trial Advocacy Training Program. This free, three-day trial advocacy course is designed to improve the trial skills of judges, public defenders, and prosecutors who appear in tribal courts. All trainings are staffed by experienced tribal prosecutors, defenders, judges, Assistant United States Attorneys (AUSAs) who prosecute Indian Country cases, and Assistant Federal Public Defenders.

Finally, the Department is also working to ensure that, in our work in Indian Country, we remain focused on providing critical services to the victims of crime. Since 2009, the Office for Victims of Crime (OVC), within the Office of Justice Programs, has provided over $2.6 million to the BIA to support victim assistance positions in Montana, South Dakota, Arizona, and New Mexico and has helped to build the capacity of sexual assault services in Indian Country through such innovative partnerships as the Department and the Indian Health Service working together to establish the American Indian/Alaska Native Sexual Assault Nurse Examiner-Sexual Assault Response Team (SANE–SART) Initiative, which addresses the comprehensive needs of tribal victims of sexual violence.

As the *Roadmap* recommends and as detailed above, the Department is embracing intergovernmental cooperation and coordination. In an effort to further strengthen the government-to-government relationships between the Department and sovereign tribes, the Department is in the process of adopting a new Statement of Principles to guide all the actions we take in working with federally recognized Indian tribes. This proposed Statement will codify our determination, as the Attorney General has remarked, to serve not as a patron, but as a partner in fighting crime and enforcing the law in Indian Country. It will also memorialize our commitment to Indian tribes and provide a foundation for reinforcing relationships, reforming the criminal justice system, and aggressively enforcing federal laws and civil rights protections. The Department has now begun the process of formal and informal consultation with tribal leaders on the Statement of Principles. [2]

Combating Domestic Violence

The fight against domestic violence in Indian Country has been an especially important priority for the Department of Justice. The Department applauds Congress for passing the bipartisan Violence Against Women Reauthorization Act of 2013 (VAWA 2013), which the President signed into law last March. This important Act, most of which has already taken effect, improves the ability of federal and tribal authorities to respond to domestic violence offenders and protect victims in three crucial ways. First, it strengthens federal domestic violence offenses and the federal assault statute—a statute frequently used in Indian Country intimate-partner violence crimes. Second, the Act recognizes the tribes' inherent power to exercise "special domestic violence criminal jurisdiction" over those who commit acts of domestic violence or dating violence or violate certain protection orders in Indian Country, regardless of their Indian or non-Indian status. Finally, it contributes to tribal self-determination by recognizing that tribes have full civil jurisdiction to issue and enforce protection orders involving any person (Indian or non-Indian) in matters arising anywhere in the tribe's Indian country or otherwise within the tribe's authority. These provisions, which help hold Indian and non-Indian perpetrators accountable, were first proposed, and have long been championed, by the Department.

While the new law's tribal criminal jurisdiction provision takes effect on March 7, 2015, VAWA 2013 also authorizes a voluntary "Pilot Project" to allow tribes to begin exercising special domestic violence criminal jurisdiction sooner. The Department received the first set of requests from six tribal governments to participate in the Pilot Project and last week three tribes—the Pascua Yaqui Tribe of Arizona, the Umatilla Tribes of Oregon, and the Tulalip Tribes of Washington—were granted Pilot Project approval by the Department. They will be the first tribes in the nation to exercise special criminal jurisdiction over crimes of domestic and dating violence, regardless of the defendant's Indian or non-Indian status, under VAWA 2013.

The *Roadmap* offers a recommendation for another step forward in Alaska as well. It urges the repeal of Section 910 of VAWA 2013. VAWA Section 910 renders the restored tribal jurisdiction provisions of Sections 904 and 905 of the Act generally inapplicable in Alaska. The Department supports the repeal of Section 910. Permitting application in Alaska of VAWA Section 905, which provides that tribes have full civil jurisdiction to issue and enforce domestic violence protection orders, would be a meaningful change that could help protect Alaska Native victims of domestic violence. Unlike VAWA Section 904 (which recognizes tribal criminal jurisdiction over certain crimes committed in a tribe's Indian country), VAWA Section 905 expressly covers not only matters arising anywhere in the tribe's Indian country but also matters that are "otherwise within the authority of the Indian tribe." So the impact of repealing Section 910 will likely have its greatest direct effect on the application of Section 905, which would then recognize Alaska tribes' civil jurisdiction to issue and enforce protection orders involving Natives and non-Natives alike.

Protecting Our Children

Providing safe, secure, and healthy communities for children is perhaps the most important priority for all stakeholders in Indian Country. In that regard, the *Roadmap* makes numerous recommendations relating to myriad criminal justice issues impacting tribal youth and juvenile justice.

---

[2] *http://www.justice.gov/tribal/*.

The Department agrees that few issues are more critical to the long-term improvement of public safety in Indian Country than working with young people to break the cycle of violence and hopelessness we have come to see on some reservations. Recognizing the importance of this issue, the Department is working to improve juvenile justice in Indian Country.

- In South Dakota, my colleague U.S. Attorney Brendan Johnson has implemented a process of collaboration with tribal prosecutors on some reservations that formalizes efforts to work together towards ensuring justice for juvenile offenders. While remaining committed to the federal prosecution of juveniles who commit the most serious offenses and those involved in gang activity, the South Dakota U.S. Attorney's Office program recognizes that, where appropriate, tribal prosecution may be the most effective method of handling juvenile misconduct. The hope is that keeping these young offenders under the supervision of the tribal court for as long as possible will provide an opportunity for rehabilitation, allow the youth to remain in his community surrounded by his family and culture, and keep federal prosecution—and a federal record—as a last resort.

- In North Dakota, in the fall of 2012, we launched a pilot program aimed at reaching young people on the Standing Rock Reservation. An AUSA in our office, who is himself an enrolled member in a North Dakota tribe, spearheaded the program. During the 2012–2013 school year, he organized a series of presentations to the student bodies of Standing Rock High School and Standing Rock Middle School designed to educate the students on protecting their personal safety and on the legal and physical/psychological hazards associated with certain conduct. The Standing Rock students were receptive to these presentations and we believe the program increased trust of the law enforcement presenters. Indeed, the *Bismarck Tribune* editorialized that "[t]o have an assistant U.S. attorney making his or her presence felt on the Standing Rock Indian Reservation—not in the courtroom but in the lives of young Native Americans—has to make a positive difference."[3] We agree.

Finally, the Department recently established the American Indian and Alaska Native Children Exposed to Violence Task Force as part of the Department's Defending Childhood Initiative. The Initiative is designed to prevent and reduce children's trauma from experiencing violence as victims or witnesses. Research funded by the Department demonstrates that a majority of America's children—more than 60 percent—are exposed to some form of violence, crime, or abuse.[4] While this study was not specific to tribal communities, our own experiences and reports from tribal leadership tell us that American Indian and Alaska Native children experience high degrees of unmet needs for services and support to prevent and respond to extreme levels of violence on some reservations.

The Task Force is made up of an Advisory Committee of tribal members and national experts—in academia, child health and trauma, and child welfare and law—and a Working Group that, along with me, includes U.S. Attorneys Amanda Marshall from Oregon, Brendan Johnson from South Dakota, and Barry Grissom from Kansas, as well as other top officials from the Departments of Justice, the Interior, and Health and Human Services. More specifically:

- The Task Force's *Advisory Committee*, co-chaired by former U.S. Senator and former chair of the Senate Committee on Indian Affairs Byron Dorgan and Iroquois composer and singer Joanne Shenandoah, has been appointed to examine the scope and impact of violence facing American Indian and Alaska Native children and make policy recommendations to Attorney General Holder on ways to address this issue.

- The *Working Group* was formed to support the Advisory Committee because the Department recognizes that there are things we can do right now that can have a direct and immediate impact in children's lives. These efforts are already making a difference. Since its inception in August 2013, the Working Group of federal officials has taken action to improve educational and programmatic services in youth detention facilities in Indian Country. Contracts have been secured for teachers who will provide educational services to Native youths held in Bureau of Indian Affairs' detention facilities.

The Advisory Committee held its first hearing on December 9, 2013, in Bismarck, North Dakota. We were honored to have Senator Heitkamp participate. Over this

---

[3] "Reaching out on the Reservation," *Bismarck Tribune*, May 3, 2012.
[4] *https://www.ncjrs.gov/pdffiles1/ojjdp/227744.pdf*

next year, the Advisory Committee will continue to travel throughout the country, holding hearings and listening sessions. The Advisory Committee will explore existing research and consult with experts to obtain a clearer picture of the incidence of violence among native children, and help identify ways to prevent it. The Advisory Committee's work will culminate in a final report—a strategic plan of action that will guide practitioners and policymakers at all levels. Similar to the work of the Defending Childhood Task Force, the recommendations of the Advisory Committee will serve as a blueprint to guide us into the future.

The work that is done in Indian Country United States Attorney's Offices across this nation every day is critical to the improvement of public safety on the reservations. As a United States Attorney who has prioritized this work in my District, I am incredibly grateful to my colleagues throughout the Department and to Attorney General Holder for their unwavering commitment to the mission in Indian Country. The United States Attorney community and the Department as a whole are proud of the work we have done thus far, but know there is much more to do. As the Attorney General has declared, we must and we will, recommit ourselves to collaboration with our tribal partners on an unprecedented scale.

Thank you for the opportunity to appear before you today to reiterate the Department's strong commitment to working with Congress, and especially this Committee, and with our tribal partners to achieve the core goals that animated the Indian Law and Order Commission and its dedicated members and staff: to build safe, sustainable, healthy, and resilient American Indian and Alaska Native communities. We praise the Commission for its hard work and devotion to strengthening and securing public safety for tribal nations, and we thank the Commission for its thoughtful and comprehensive recommendations.

I look forward to answering any questions you may have.

The CHAIRWOMAN. Thank you. And again, I thank both the witnesses.

I am going to start with you, Assistant Secretary Washburn. One of the goals of the high priority performance goal was to target a 35 percent reduction, and these pilots have come back with some pretty spectacular results.

So what does the Administration plan on doing to expand the program? Are you looking at the fiscal year 2015 budget? What do we know about what might be needed as far as a budget number to help address this on a larger scale than just these pilots?

Mr. WASHBURN. Thank you, Madam Chairwoman. We have found that those pilots were indeed very successful. I think that what they show is that when we invest appropriate resources we get results. I think that that is now clear.

We are moving forward with similar pilot programs like that in other places in Indian Country. What we will be doing going forward is expanding what we are trying to do to address public safety more holistically so that we are addressing, we are going to create a program that will give tribes the ability to use the money where they think best. If it is substance abuse, or other areas, reentry, we would like to expand sort of the idea of HPPG, which is that if we invest money, we will get results. But we want to try to decrease recidivism. Rather than going straight at the crime rate, we are going to start trying to get the recidivism rate, repeat offenders.

So that is kind of the next step for that program. I can't talk too much about actual funding requests going forward for 2015, although the Committee usually does have a hearing in late March after the budget comes out. So I will be able to speak more about that when the final decisions have been made. So we can talk, going forward, about the funding at that time.

The CHAIRWOMAN. Okay. How about something a little more basic. You do believe that you should expand the pilot programs?

Mr. WASHBURN. Well, yes. We have seen success. That is the bottom line. The question, I think now, we have some difficult fiscal challenges, because if we can do this well at four locations, we do have 566 tribes. So there are some fiscal challenges to expanding this to all tribes. So we need to figure out how to go forward in light of those fiscal challenges. But the exercise has proven itself, that when we invest well and invest strategically we can make a difference.

The CHAIRWOMAN. On this question of special prosecutors, Mr. Purdon, you basically painted them in a pretty positive light. Very much walking in both worlds and making it work. So I was surprised that one of the commission's findings that the FBI Office of Justice Services and U.S. Attorneys' office are reluctant to provide Federal criminal investigation information to the deputized prosecutors.

Mr. PURDON. Right.

The CHAIRWOMAN. So is that your experience with them? What should we do about trying to solve that problem?

Mr. PURDON. That is not my experience in North Dakota. And I can speak more broadly first. I think the Department has seen that recommendation from the Committee, is it the intention of the Department that Special Assistant United States Attorneys who have passed a background check and who can go into court and represent the United States of America, that they are entitled to the sensitive law enforcement information they need to work on the cases that they are prosecuting.

So that is the Department's position. To the extent that that might not be happening in a couple of spots, we are committed to making sure that does happen. In North Dakota, our experience has been the opposite, that once those SAUSAs become certified and become part of my team at the U.S. Attorney's office, they go into court shoulder to shoulder with our AUSAs. We treat them like AUSAs. We don't, in North Dakota, keep information from them. They are part of the team.

It is that collaboration between the assistant U.S. Attorneys, the line prosecutors in my office that have dedicated their lives to making Indian Country safer and the tribes own representative, the tribal prosecutor, who has that joint interest in public safety on the reservation. Bringing those two forces together, it helps get convictions but it also increases the communication and the collaboration and the idea, we really become then more community prosecutors, become part of that community.

My folks live in Bismarck. They don't live in Fort Yates on the reservation. But our goal is to make those AUSAs part of that community so that they are involved in the public safety challenges of that reservation.

The CHAIRWOMAN. Thank you. So, share information.

Mr. PURDON. That is the goal. That is what we do. That is the position of the Department of Justice.

The CHAIRWOMAN. Thank you. I have more questions but I will let my colleagues here have some time, we will go back and forth.

The Vice Chairman stepped out for a while. Senator Murkowski, do you have a question?

STATEMENT OF HON. LISA MURKOWSKI,
U.S. SENATOR FROM ALASKA

Senator MURKOWSKI. I do, Madam Chairman. Thank you for advancing this very important discussion today. Welcome, too, to our witnesses. I haven't had a chance to hear your verbal testimony but I have read your written statements and appreciate that.

Quick question for you, Secretary Washburn. The BIA has made it a policy of not funding tribal courts or law enforcement, in Public Law 280 States. So given that what we are seeing from the Commission in terms of a recommendation, would the BIA be willing to submit a budget request to Congress that includes funding for tribes in Public Law 280 States?

Mr. WASHBURN. Thank you for that question, Senator Murkowski. It is a very difficult question.

Senator MURKOWSKI. I know it is. It seems so easy to ask. Put this in the budget.

[Laughter.]

Mr. WASHBURN. Thank you for recognizing that. The problem is, it is sort of a simple fiscal problem, which is that we don't necessarily have enough money to do everything the Federal Government needs to do for every constituency. And so we don't—I think we have an existing system where we have only, we have exclusive responsibility with the tribes, the Federal Government and the tribes, in ordinary Indian Country type jurisdictions. In Public Law 280 States, the States have a responsibility and a delegation of Federal authority.

We feel like we need to focus our funding where it is most needed, which is in those jurisdictions where the tribes and Federal Government have exclusive jurisdiction. That is not a policy decision. It is just a necessity based on limited fiscal resources.

I guess I would say I can't fully answer your question because the question would, especially under the Murray-Ryan budget scenario we have, we have to figure out where we would take the money from to fund Public Law 280 law enforcement States, tribes in those States. And that is a difficult question. So we have a limited amount of money, and where do we take it from is the question.

Senator MURKOWSKI. I understand that, because we are dealing with that every day up here. But I also recognize that as I am talking with tribes from Alaska that truly are trying to make the best of an already squeezed situation; they are not asking for a lot. They are asking for some level of contribution and participation. And as we know, they are taking up that responsibility and yet the compensation or the reimbursement for them is slim to none.

Extraordinarily challenging for them, and yet they are stepping forward and doing the best job that they can. We have got to be creative. This is where, Mr. Purdon, I appreciate what you, the perspective that you provide, coming from the U.S. Attorneys office and the efforts that we are working on to be more collaborative, cross-deputization, how we are looking critically at how we do better, given our very, very difficult budget considerations.

I also appreciate the clarification that you provided on section 910 of VAWA. I think there is a lot of confusion about what Alaska tribes are eligible for or not eligible for. And I obviously absolutely support the policy that our tribal court protective orders over our members or non-members in relationship with tribal members are honored. And in fact, the State of Alaska has confirmed that these protective orders are honored once they are registered. It is important to make sure that that is more clarified.

A couple of questions then for you. This task force, the American Indian Alaska Native Children Exposed to Violence Task Force, I know that you are going to be, well, I guess I want to know if the task force will be visiting Alaska. Valerie Davidson, of course, is on that task force and always represents us well. But do you have plans to go to the State?

Mr. PURDON. Yes. The Alaska Native American Indian Children Exposed to Violence Federal Advisory Committee, which is part of our task force, along with the working group that I am part of, that advisory committee held its first hearing in Bismarck. We were honored to have Senator Heitkamp speak at that hearing. They met this week, Assistant Secretary Washburn was in Phoenix for the second meeting. The third meeting, the location is escaping me, but my understanding is that there is a commitment for that fourth meeting, that it will take place in Alaska.

Senator MURKOWSKI. Great. That is good to hear.

This is just a much broader question and not fair, as I have just allowed the clock to go to zero, but how do you see an expanded role of U.S. Attorneys in rural Alaska? Are there some partnerships that we can create with our tribes and our State to really better serve, what can we be doing better there?

Mr. PURDON. Obviously unlike myself in North Dakota, where I have primary jurisdiction over major crimes in Indian Country, the situation is different in Alaska. Obviously you understand that, but just to set the stage.

That being said, the U.S. Attorney's office in Alaska, along with Federal law enforcement agencies, is taking, I think, some concrete steps to assist the remote villages that are the subject of the report and the subject of your concern. For instance, the FBI and the U.S. Attorneys office conducts a great deal, my understanding is, of outreach to the villages on the issue of sex trafficking. Because there is a vulnerable population of young people in those communities. The FBI has a project, Innocence Lost, I believe, and a partnership with the U.S. Attorneys office. That outreach and training has been done. So that is something we can do, even though the U.S. Attorneys office doesn't have jurisdiction over the villages.

Additionally, in 2012, the U.S. Attorneys office, my colleague Karen Loeffler in Alaska, applied for and received funding for a specific AUSA in her office to focus on violent crime in rural Alaska. Now, that person doesn't have major crimes jurisdiction, but they have been able to make use of existing Federal authorities under perhaps the drug or the firearms titles to charge and prosecute under Federal law folks that are violent criminals out in rural Alaska, including the villages. That is an important step, and one that should be recognized. Then I also understand that the U.S. Marshal Service and the U.S. Attorneys office work hard with the villages in terms of sex offender registration and ensuring that people pay penalties if they don't register.

So in addition to the U.S. Attorneys office, the Office of Justice Programs does offer financial support as well. The Native villages are eligible for our CTAS grants, and there is grant money that flows to those villages as well. So we have to do what we can with the resources and the prosecutorial techniques we have. U.S. Attorney Loeffler is an active member of our subcommittee and is committed to this issue. They have done what they can, given the jurisdictional hurdles.

Senator MURKOWSKI. It has really helped to have the participant of the marshals, too, and just having an extra presence. So cumulatively, you try to chip away at it. It is a big problem and I appreciate your comments.

Thank you, Madam Chair.

[The prepared statement of Senator Murkowski follows:]

PREPARED STATEMENT OF HON. LISA MURKOWSKI, U.S. SENATOR FROM ALASKA

I would like to thank Chairman Cantwell and Vice Chairman Barrasso for the scheduling this hearing on the Indian Law and Order Commission Report. I was a proud co-sponsor of the Tribal Law and Order Act of 2010, a bill that authorized the Indian Law and Order Commission to do its work. I would like to thank the Commission for their hard work and extensive outreach to Indian country and Alaska Native villages—often the most rural and untraveled parts of America.

While we appreciate that the Commission has directed attention to the shameful statistics and reality of public safety in rural Alaska, the recommendations have generated much controversy in our state—fueling a long standing historical debate over the Alaska Native Land Claims Settlement Act, and whether or not tribes should have reservation trust lands. The Commissioners have addressed the issue of public safety in Alaska from the lens of Indian country, rather than those working to address the barriers to justice in our villages.

In rural Alaska, the barriers to delivering justice are tremendous—not only geographic, but also financial. I have been driving a conversation of partnership between the State and our tribes. Whether it be through the construction of public safety buildings, holding cells and health clinics, or through providing training for tribal law enforcement and honoring tribal court protective orders—cooperation is necessary. The fact of the matter is, we all must be asking more of ourselves—the Tribes, the State, and the Federal Government.

What concerns me, is that often a young women who is sexually assaulted in a village must be flown hundreds of miles away to a hub community like Bethel, Nome or Anchorage, for a forensic exam and for evidence to be collected for prosecution. This only happens if she is willing to report what has happened to her—because the experience of too many others is that nothing will happen to her perpetrator. Our young women cannot be afraid to speak out, for fear of local politics or retribution.

What protocols and relationships between our tribes and the State need to occur? What role must our health providers play to address domestic violence and sexual assault in our communities? What can we be doing in the area of prevention, with our school districts? What are we collectively doing to address the deplorable housing conditions? What are we doing to make sure a woman, and often her children, have options when they leave a women's shelter?

These are the questions we must ask in order to drive the conversation that I hope to have in Alaska. There are good examples. In the AVCP region last year, the regional tribal organization and the State of Alaska partnered to build three new public safety buildings in Kalskag, Mekoryuk, and Russian Mission. AVCP, in partnership with the State will build new public safety buildings in Aniak, Kwigillingok, Mountain Village, and Tununak. All hire is local, which provides added economic boost for families in the region.

Our regional tribal organization based in Dillingham, Alaska has created a prisoner re-entry program for Native men who leave prison. The Bristol Bay Native Association, with outreach to the Alaska Department of Corrections, the Alaska Juvenile Justice Program, and the National Reentry Resource Center has created the

Bristol Bay Regional Reentry Coalition to help those released with employment, housing, children and culture.

The Indian Law and Order Commission Report—failed to examine what works in rural Alaska when it comes to achieving public safety and the partnerships that exist between our regional tribal non-profits, including our tribal health providers and the State of Alaska. Instead, the report took aim to the long-standing battle of whether or not Alaska should have Indian reservations.

In the 2013 Violence Against Women Act, I asked the Attorney General of the United States, the State of Alaska, and the Alaska Federation of Natives to revisit the purpose and composition of the Alaska Rural Justice and Law Enforcement Commission. I look forward to hearing from Alaskans on how we collectively will address the issue of public safety in Alaska.

The CHAIRWOMAN. Thank you. Senator Heitkamp?

Senator HEITKAMP. Thank you, Madam Chairwoman. Just a quick point, and I think that the Honorable Kevin Washburn is tired of me saying this. But obviously we now have the report. We are waiting to find out what the Administration's fiscal response is to that, and we look forward to seeing the Presidential budget, because we hope that it reflects the great need that we see for law enforcement and for law and order in Indian Country. So I will just lay down my marker, we are waiting. We will wait and see.

My questions are mainly for U.S. Attorney Tim Purdon. Obviously those of us who have done this work over a long period of time realize that we can in fact continue to invest resources, continue to do what we are doing. But so much of what happens is related to substance abuse, drug and alcohol addiction. In fact a rate of over, I think it is 220 percent of all, over another DOJ statistical average is what we see in Indian Country related to alcohol. So let's not kid ourselves. Because we have a chronic addiction issue, we have recidivism. That recidivism not only takes a lot of prosecutorial effort, but it continues to add to the despair and dismembering, really, of the community.

So my question is, what are you doing to promote re-entry programs in tribal communities in order to combat recidivism?

Mr. PURDON. Senator Heitkamp, re-entry is a huge challenge. Ninety-five percent of the folks that my AUSAs prosecute and send to Federal prison, 95 percent of them come back to the reservation at some point. This is an issue that is very personal to me. Before I was U.S. Attorney, Senator Heitkamp, as you are aware, I was in private practice. I actually did some public defender work and defended folks charged with crimes in Federal court.

I had a client once that I had represented and he went to prison and I ran into him at the halfway house in Bismarck seven years later. He is coming out of prison. You never know how those conversations are going to go. But he was happy to see me and I said, oh, how are you doing? He said, I am doing well, I am at the halfway house, I have a job, I have a sponsor, I am in an AA group and I have a sponsor and things were going well for him in Bismarck. But he is not from Bismarck. He is from Standing Rock. And when his six months were up at the halfway house, he got in a car and went back to Standing Rock. Three months later, I got a call, his probation is being revoked, he is being sent back to Federal prison.

I said to him, what happened? He said, well, I got back to Standing Rock, no job, no AA group, no sponsor. And we see that over and over and over again. So re-entry has to be part, besides just the prosecution side, we have to get involved in re-entry. And so one of the challenges we have, we don't have halfway house facilities where inmates can do their last six months of BOP custody on the reservations. They are doing these halfway house stints hundreds of miles from their home.

That is not something I can impact. But what I can impact, and I have worked hard within the Department, I actually chair the Federal Interagency Re-Entry Council's Working Group on Re-Entry in Indian Country. We have to figure out how to make, re-entry is a big part of the attorney generals' agenda right now. What about that Indian Country piece?

And we need to do more, I am working, in North Dakota, working closely with the court, with the probation office, to see how we can work together to provide some sort of support for those folk coming back.

Senator HEITKAMP. And I would add to your challenge re-entry of Native American kids who come in and out of juvenile justice facilities and then have absolutely no support when they return home.

Mr. PURDON. Absolutely.

Senator HEITKAMP. Just a quick story, when I started as attorney general, I wrote an opinion. It was based on a Montana court case which said States' attorneys don't have jurisdiction in certain situations. We went, along with the State court officials, went to the Department of Justice, not Justice, but we went to the courts and said, look, we need to expand our part-time magistrate to be a full-time magistrate. Our vision was that that magistrate would actually be a circuit rider and would take court onto the reservations so that we didn't have transportation issues, you have a clearer vision of how this works, people can come down and watch, it is not hundreds of miles away.

Mr. PURDON. Right.

Senator HEITKAMP. You know what? That never happened. And so often, what we have is we have no court system that we are working with right on site. So what can the Attorney General do to expand Federal court presence on reservations along with collaboration with tribal courts?

Mr. PURDON. What can the attorney general do? He can't do as much as the AO of the U.S. court system, right. But in North Dakota, we have worked creatively and we have a sweep, and this has occurred, we had an operation, Prairie Thunder, at Standing Rock, where we had a sweep of some folk accused of drug crimes. The magistrate came down to Standing Rock and stayed the night. The Federal magistrate from Bismarck came down, held court behind a table in the gym at Standing Rock. We need to be, we as U.S. Attorneys, need to be working with the courts to try and do more of that sort of thing, of bringing the Federal court, making it relevant. To somebody in Fort Yates, well, Fort Yates isn't that far, but Belcourt, what goes on in Bismarck, 200 miles away, it just creates such great challenges all the way around.

Senator HEITKAMP. And I really encourage you to work within the court system, and I think we should create an expectation in the Congress that, look, we understand you like your Federal courthouses and that you have a lot of security. But you also have an obligation here, especially related to major crimes, when you bring it, and people can see that there are consequences, that has an effect, too.

Mr. PURDON. Absolutely.

Senator HEITKAMP. So we will continue to work on the issue of access to justice by locating courts where people live.

The CHAIRWOMAN. Thank you. Vice Chairman Barrasso?

Senator BARRASSO. Thank you very much, Madam Chairwoman.

Secretary Washburn, Ivan Posey, who wasn't able to be here today, council member for a long time, Eastern Shoshone Tribe in Wyoming, long-time advocate for Native youth, I just wanted to visit a little bit about that. He submitted written testimony for this hearing, recommending that stronger preventive services be provided to reduce the unacceptably high number of Native youth who are entering the justice system. I just wondered if there are things that you thought of what the Department of the Interior could do to assist in preventing Native youth from entering the justice system.

Mr. WASHBURN. I think that is an important question. There are a lot of services that we need to be providing. Crime doesn't exist in a vacuum. Someone let the child down if they are in that situation, somewhere along the line. And it may have been a lot of people who let that child down. So there certainly are a lot of things we can do.

This new approach that we are looking forward to implementing, a pilot project with some specific tribes to try to provide more of those wraparound services to prevent recidivism and prevent offending, and giving the tribes the tools they need to deal with substance abuse and other issues like that, will be an effort to do those things. You are absolutely right, that we need to prevent crimes before they happen.

I spent a few years as a Federal prosecutor. It was very apparent to me as I prosecuted juveniles and adult defendants that the problem that led to this crime happened usually many years before I ran across them. And so it made me think that we can't prosecute our way out of criminal problems on reservations. We need to be thinking much more broadly than that. So I certainly agree with what you are suggesting.

Senator BARRASSO. Mr. Purdon, when I look at the Commission report, it seems that the Native American youth are significantly over-represented in the juvenile justice system. These youths seem to receive harsher sentences. You are nodding your head, you are well aware of that of the finding.

The Commission recommended Federal pre-trial diversion programs that allow sentencing in the tribal court. Can you talk a little bit about what other efforts there might be that we could undertake or you could through the Department of Justice?

Mr. PURDON. Two programs, two pilots, two things to think about. My colleague in South Dakota, United States Attorney Brendan Johnson, has been a real leader on this issue in South Dakota. His office has been able to strike some MOUs with some of the tribes with developed court systems whereby a Native American juvenile offender who might get sucked into Federal court, they are able to work with the tribal court and put that person, put that young person on tribal probation. And if they successfully complete the probation under the tribal court umbrella, they are not prosecuted in Federal court.

Obviously, there has to be a balance. I see some juvenile offenders who come across my desk who have committed horrific crimes, committed homicide, they have committed sexual assault. So there has to be a balance there as well. But for someone who is not involved in that sort of a conduct, the South Dakota Johnson model is a great model. I have asked my prosecutors to take a look at that, should we be implementing something similar perhaps with Standing Rock that has a very well developed court system, where we can trust the probation officers are going to do a good job of monitoring that American Indian youth.

See, that is one thing. In my office I am tremendously proud of the work of one of my AUSAs, a man named Gary Delorme, who is an enrolled member of one of our reservations himself. He is in charge of the Standing Rock Reservation. Over the last two years, he and the tribal prosecutor have met on a monthly basis at the high school with high school and middle school students to talk about staying away from drugs, wearing your seat belt. He has brought in Native American law enforcement officers to talk about their career path. And Gary reports to me that when juvenile cases come to his desk now and he goes to a court appearance with one of those kids who sat in those meetings with him, that young man is embarrassed that he is now in front of Gary in a juvenile court proceeding. Gary has become part of his life. It goes back to what I saying to Senator Cantwell about becoming a member of that community.

That is a program that has worked for us. It may work in other jurisdictions. But the resources of the U.S. Attorneys office on the reservation, not just prosecuting cases, but becoming a part of that community and spending the resources that we have, expanding them to the reservation, that has to have a positive impact. So there are two examples. I think your point is well taken. When we look at the number of Native American youth, look at the number of juveniles in our Federal system, they are almost all Native American. That is because of the jurisdictional challenge.

The BOP, they have a job. And this is a very difficult situation. We need to create and find ways to help these folk without, where appropriate, pulling them into that Federal system. So I agree with you.

Senator BARRASSO. Thank you, Madam Chairwoman.

The CHAIRWOMAN. Senator Begich?

Senator BEGICH. Thank you very much. Thanks to both of you for being here. I have a few questions here. Let me first follow up if I can, Mr. Washburn, always good to see you. Thank you very much for being here.

You made a comment, I want to follow through on a couple things here. You made the comment, the statement, equal partners. So let me ask you, and I know there was a question from my colleague, Senator Murkowski, regarding BIA tribal justice funds and the complication of funding levels. So let me say, from first to base point, and that is, are there any restrictions, not money, regulatory, legislatively or otherwise, to restrict State of Alaska tribes from accessing these grant monies?

Mr. WASHBURN. Senator Begich, that is a legal question. I am not positive that I know the answer to it. I don't believe that there are restrictions, at least for self-governance and 638 type monies. I don't know if there are restrictions as to grant monies. But we can look into that and get back to you. It is more of a policy decision at the Department of Justice.

Senator BEGICH. I understand. I wanted to make sure there is nothing illegal. Mr. Purdon, were you about to say something on that?

Mr. PURDON. The Coordinated Tribal Assistance Grants that we send out, my understanding is that Alaska villages receive those monies. I checked on that before we started.

Senator BEGICH. I understand that piece, but the other piece is the tribal justice funds from BIA. Don't worry, I have a question for you.

[Laughter.]

Senator BEGICH. So if you could find out, first, if there is a restriction.

Now to the second part of the question, let's assume for a moment there are no restrictions. The question then is, how big of a pie do you have to have in order for Alaskan tribes to access that money if the issue is money versus legal or legislative? You may not be able to answer that question right now, so I want to understand that.

Mr. WASHBURN. Let me just tell you, I can't answer the question specifically, but let me put it in context, because we do have, as Senator Murkowski said, 229 Alaska villages, that is a lot. We also have about 100 tribes in California that are also Public Law 280 tribes that don't have this kind of funding. So if you do it for Alaska, maybe you need to do it for California too.

So those are issues, we had a tribe come in a couple of days ago.

Senator BEGICH. Well, that is at least three appropriators, so keep going.

[Laughter.]

Mr. WASHBURN. That is exactly the political battle, I suppose. And so there are a lot of tribes that want this and they could do good things with this money if we could find the money.

Senator BEGICH. What I would like you to do if you could, if there is not a report done or some document that says, here is the current capacity, here is what is needed by the current folks that are using the money and here is what the potential might be, I know it would be broad ranges. But if we don't know the numbers, we don't know what we are working with. Is that something you could work on or get to us?

Mr. WASHBURN. We can work on that, yes, sir.

Senator BEGICH. Okay. Let me go back to the CTAS monies, the Coordinated Tribal Assistance Solicitation dollars. Again, Alaska tribes can apply for them. But here is the question that I have. Can that money be used for executing the implementation of inter-governmental agreements between the State and the tribes? Why I ask this, let me give you the precursor. I have a piece of legislation pending on the Safe Villages and Families Act, which talks about coordination. I wish the Act was much stronger and will look for your recommendations, to be frank with you, on how we can strengthen the current piece of legislation we have on the table. But putting that aside, it talks about this coordination. Can they apply for grants through this, CTAS, and use to develop these coordinations and efforts with the State?

Mr. PURDON. I wonder what you mean by executing implementation or entering into these. Certainly they can, the monies that come to them, there is certainly no limitation that you can't then enter into an MOU.

Senator BEGICH. No, the way we draft this legislation, again, I want it stronger, but it is what it is. And it basically talks about the tribe and the State negotiating an agreement.

Mr. PURDON. Right.

Senator BEGICH. That takes resources before you get to the agreement. So the question is, can those resources be used to help the tribe have these technical assistance and everything to help negotiate against a pretty big organization, the State of Alaska, which honestly has not been very favorable to my legislation. So do you see where I am going?

Mr. PURDON. Yes, I do. I will get back to you. I will say that the idea of increasing or encouraging coordination through MOU between State and county governments and the tribes, absolutely.

Senator BEGICH. That is one of your goals.

Mr. PURDON. That is one of the goals. We struggle with it in North Dakota. I try and bring local law enforcement and the tribes together, listening conferences and getting together. At the end of the day, though, as the Federal Government, I can't make them do anything.

Senator BEGICH. So you understand the question, if you could get that back to us?

Mr. PURDON. I will get back to you on that.

Senator BEGICH. So this is a quick yes or no. I think your testimony may have had this in it, both of you. As you know, my legislation, Safe Families and Villages Act, has a repeal to Section 910 of VAWA. Do you support that repeal or not?

Mr. WASHBURN. I think I can speak for both of us. We both support that repeal. I think I heard from Senator Murkowski that she supports repeal of that section as well. That would be low-hanging fruit for a new Chairman of the Senate Committee on Indian Affairs, if we got the Republican Member from Alaska and the Democrat Senator from Alaska.

Senator BEGICH. That is legislation we are both on. So we will find that right person and have that discussion. But you both are in favor of repealing that?

Mr. PURDON. The Department absolutely supports that.

Senator BEGICH. Okay. I will finish there, Madam Chair, thank you.

The CHAIRWOMAN. Senator Tester, you seem to be up.

STATEMENT OF HON. JON TESTER,
U.S. SENATOR FROM MONTANA

Senator TESTER. In more ways than one. Thank you both for being here. I appreciate the opportunity to visit with you, Kevin, always. And Tim, it is good to see you again. You may not be getting out tonight.

I want to follow up on the MOU conversation with you. Is there more Congress can do on this issue?

Mr. PURDON. That is a good question, and I don't know the answer off the top of my head. But I think that it is hard, it is hard, I have found this to be a difficult part of my job over the last three and a half years. I have sat in the county courthouse in Rolette County in North Dakota with the BIA police chief and the sheriff. And they all say, yes, we should do this, we need a go-by. Here is a go-by. I will give you a go-by. But there we are.

And I think there is a history of some of these places that we just have to keep chipping away and getting people in the same room and communicating. I don't know what Congress can do to encourage that.

Senator TESTER. When you are out in the field, if you think of some stuff, I think there are some real benefits to being able to have folk work together and communicate well.

Senator Heitkamp talked about recidivism. You talked about the fact that the chap you knew had a sponsor, went to AA and had a job, went back to the reservation and there was none of the above. What is possible here, Kevin, and Tim, as far as that goes; is there an infrastructure out there to be able to do some modifications, or are we starting from ground zero? Because you are absolutely right, if you lose all those tools, you get back in the same climate that got you in trouble to begin with.

Mr. PURDON. Here is what I found after 18 months of studying this, is that state of the art is the Boston re-entry model, David Kennedy's model of combining an offender coming out, some law enforcement or person of authority meets with them and says, careful or you are going to get revoked, and then here are these services that are available, you need your GED, you need job training.

What I have found is that I have had colleagues that have begun very successful reentry programs in southern Alabama and larger urban areas, and there is a support network, maybe churches. On the reservation, that piece has been very difficult to figure out a way to bring that panoply of services to the table. So that is a challenge. But that goes back to the idea of crime prevention, holistic approach, the same thing we have been talking about.

Senator TESTER. Let's talk about prevention. You talked about education a minute ago with one of the questions. What other preventive services are out there that could really work?

Mr. PURDON. Well, my answer is this. What I have done—I don't have a catalog of preventive services I can just impact on a reservation. What I have done is get my AUSAs on the reservation with their ears open, so if they hear about a viable crime prevention program we can figure out a way to support it. Gary's program of talking to the schools is one of these.

But we just have to be creative. It becomes getting our folks out of the office in Bismarck and Fargo and onto the reservation on a more frequent basis, to become part of the community. That is what we can do, keep our ears open. And when we see something that looks like it is going to work that the tribe is interested in, come and figure out a way to support it.

Senator TESTER. This is for both, if you want to answer it. The Department has implemented some VAWA pilot projects rather quickly. I commend you on that. What is the expansion plan for these pilot projects?

Mr. PURDON. I have been part of the team that has been working on reviewing the applications and launching these pilot projects. So there are the three tribes that were approved, I think it was last week, to begin, Tulalip, Umatilla and Pascua Yaqui. There are other tribes whose applications are pending in our review, and they are free to continue to apply. I don't know if I have answered your question, but it is an ongoing process.

Senator TESTER. I was just wondering, is there a plan for expanding the pilots.

Mr. PURDON. Yes. Tribes continue to apply, continue to be reviewed. If there are tribes whose application come in today and they are ready to go, the Department will continue to approve.

Mr. WASHBURN. Yes, and Senator Tester, every tribe will have the opportunity to do this, come March of 2015. So they don't need to go through a pilot period first.

Senator TESTER. Thanks. Declination rates, very, very quickly. Can you give me an update on the rate of declination in Indian Country? Where are we?

Mr. PURDON. Sir, the Indian Country Investigation and Prosecution Report that came to Congress last spring has the most recent numbers in terms of prosecutions being up over 50 percent and the corresponding declination rates.

Senator TESTER. Up 50 percent over what?

Mr. PURDON. So from 2009, the number of Indian Country cases prosecuted by U.S. Attorneys across the Country in 2009 was around 1,110. In 2013, it was well over 1,600. So the raw number of criminal cases filed on the reservations is up over 54 percent. In North Dakota, we have seen similar increases. I think the number of defendants we have charged since 2009 is up 48 percent, the number of cases is up over 80 percent. With that, we have seen a corresponding decrease in our declination rate.

Senator TESTER. How many cases are being declined?

Mr. PURDON. We cut our declination in North Dakota, our rate in half.

Senator TESTER. So how many cases are being declined?

Mr. PURDON. I don't have the number off the top of my head. But the number of cases we are doing is way up and our declination rate is down.

Senator TESTER. I appreciate that, I do, Tim. I don't mean to be a terrible human being. But an issue around declination in Indian Country, until it matches up to the declination rate outside of Indian Country, we should not be happy. You can tell me I am wrong.

Mr. PURDON. Well, you have heard this, there are lots of reasons to decline a case. But let me think of one thing that happened in North Dakota that changed the way I thought about this a little bit. Because when I came in, this was three and a half years ago, this was an issue that concerned me. We had this Operation Prairie Thunder down at Standing Rock where we scooped up 21 guys, and many of them had prior drug offenses, so they got charged in Federal court. There were three or four of these guys, though, that were 19 years old. It was their first offense. Because we had tribal SAUSAs at Standing Rock and because we were working closely with them on this whole operation, we made the decision to charge those four or five guys in tribal court.

Now, I am proud of those referrals. That was the right thing to do. Historically, those would have been treated as a declination.

Senator TESTER. Oh, really? Okay. That is good information.

Mr. PURDON. Yes, historically.

Senator TESTER. Thank you both.

The CHAIRWOMAN. Thank you, Senator Tester. I am trying to be liberal here with the clock, just because, well, first of all, I am so impressed with my colleagues for being here. I think a lot of people throw barbs at Congress at what we get done, but here it is, about to be a snowstorm, people are running to catch planes and here are six of my colleagues who are here paying attention to a very——

Senator MURKOWSKI. Look at where we're from.

[Laughter.]

Senator TESTER. We aren't going anywhere.

The CHAIRWOMAN. Nonetheless, you could still be doing something else, and I think from the tone and detail of your questions, people can see that you all care passionately about this issue and you are trying to make this a focal point of what can we do better. Again, I thank our witnesses on this panel, because obviously this report highlights what we can do better and you are making some suggestions. So then we are going to hold you both to the budget issues and these recommendations. But we definitely have to move forward. I thank you for the creativity and success you have shown so far.

But these Members are here because it affects every one of them and their States. And it affects the people of their State. I do appreciate them being here.

Let's move on to the second panel. We are going to hear from Mr. Troy Eid, who is the Chairman of the Indian Law and Order Commission, from Denver, Colorado; Ms. Affie Ellis, who is the Commissioner of Indian Law and Order Commission, from Cheyenne, Wyoming; and Ms. Tamra Truett Jerue, who is the Director of Social Services and Tribal Administrator from Anvik Tribal Counsel, Anvik, Alaska.

Welcome to all of you. Thank you for being here, thank you for your patience this afternoon. We will start with you, Ms. Ellis.

STATEMENT OF AFFIE ELLIS, COMMISSIONER, INDIAN LAW AND ORDER COMMISSION

Ms. ELLIS. Thank you, Madam Chair. I want to thank everyone for the opportunity for us to be here to present our work.

My name is Affie Ellis. I am a member of the Navajo Nation and I am also a citizen of Wyoming. I was appointed to the Commission by Senator Minority Leader Mitch McConnell. It has been an honor for me to serve on this commission.

I want to thank my fellow Commissioners. I know you are watching online and we certainly wish you were here with us today.

I also want to pay special thanks to all the people that we met in the field over the course of the last three years. They have shared with us some very personal and sometimes very difficult information. It wasn't always easy to hear what they had to say, but we appreciate your candor and your honesty.

As has been noted very much today, there have been a lot of efforts to make Native America safer and more just. I want to thank all the Members of this Committee for being here and for supporting those efforts. In particular, I want to thank Senator Barrasso for supporting my nomination to this Commission and for supporting our hearing today. Wyoming is very lucky to have you.

When we first met to work on our report, we didn't know what the final product was going to look like. But we had a few guiding principles. First, we pledged to listen to the people that we met. And it was these people who defined the scope of what we talked about in our report.

We were also interested in writing a report that said something, that actually said something, and wouldn't just be a document that sat on a shelf accumulating dust. By the end of our field hearings, when we started putting pen to paper, we decided we wanted to speak with a unified voice. We didn't want a report that had a majority recommendation with dissenting views. And the reason for this is very simple: these issues are too important. In short, people are dying, people are suffering, and our report was written in a unified voice with those people in mind.

Indian Country Today, as many of you have seen, wrote a story about our report, and they described it as radical, revolutionary, exceptional or just plain common sense. And I am not a fancy gal, I am a nice Navajo person from Wyoming, so I like the term common sense to best describe our recommendations and our work. In short, we called for more local, tribal control over law enforcement issues.

When we were out in the field, we saw a lot of bright spots where tribes were working with State and Federal partners. They had invested in hiring more tribal police, they invested in detention facilities to meet the needs of their citizens. They were investing in tribal courts that were familiar with their clients, as our fellow Commissioner, Judge Pouley, likes to call defendants before her court. And they paid close attention to rehabilitation needs.

When the Commission saw areas where things were working, we kept hearing one thing over and over: look what we are doing. Rarely did we hear, actually I would say never did we hear, look what other people, the Federal Government, is doing for us.

Our Commission thus views tribal governments as playing the lead role in strengthening tribal justice. We recognize that tribes have a lot of challenges and that they have got to continue to develop internal capacities to become more self-determinant across all tribal justice functions. This isn't easy, we know this, but it can and must be done. Lack of law enforcement remains a problem in many places in Indian Country, particularly Alaska. We know boots-on-the-ground law enforcement is essential for reducing crime. Our report talks about HPPG, and how increased law enforcement in certain areas has made a difference. In other words, it is saving lives.

We all know, though, that increasing law enforcement and other services requires funding. Accordingly, we recommend structural changes within the Federal Government to reduce confusion and redundancy by transferring law enforcement duties within the Department of Interior to the Department of Justice. Our report highlights one instance where DOJ funds were available to build a detention facility in Indian Country, but the building sat empty because no funds were appropriated through the DOI budget.

We also recommend base level funding after repeatedly hearing about how grant-based funding is not a good match for Indian Country's needs. Some tribes, we have heard, struggle to write the winning application because they don't have the human capital to complete those applications. And more problematically, we hear about grants coming and going, because a program will get money and then run out of funds.

But I think what is most troubling is that grants reflect the Federal Government's idea about what works in Indian Country, rather than trusting tribes to make those decisions on their own. Our report is very lengthy, and I do want to apologize that my good friend, Ivan Posey, could not be here today. He provided some very meaningful testimony about some efforts at Wind River to address juvenile justice. We urge the Committee to continue to look at our report with a fine-toothed comb to see what works in your particular areas. And we want to thank all the tribes that welcomed us to their reservations, and particularly Alaska. We visited some extremely remote villages and were welcomed by very gracious people.

So while we have huge challenges that remain, I just want to thank everyone for your continued interest and commitment to reducing crime in Native America and Native Alaska villages. Thank you so much and I am just going to say, I appreciate the opportunity to present before my esteemed colleague, the Chairman of the Commission, Troy Eid. Thank you.

The CHAIRWOMAN. Thank you.

Sir, I thank you very much. I appreciate your being here and thank you for your leadership on the Commission.

STATEMENT OF TROY A. EID, CHAIRMAN, INDIAN LAW AND ORDER COMMISSION

Mr. EID. Thank you, Madam Chair. I sure do appreciate it, and Mr. Vice Chair, good to see you. I appreciate all your support, Committee members.

My name is Troy Eid, from Denver, Colorado. I wanted to try to find a way to thank you and express my concern. All I can say is, but for this Committee, there would be no report. When you are appointed to a Committee like this, or a commission, there is no instruction manual. It was the staff of this Committee that stepped forward and said, here is how you get this done. I am very grateful to all of you and I want to express that publicly.

I also thank our other commission members. We are all volunteers. We spent three years of our lives doing this. We have come up with the most comprehensive report probably ever on this subject matter. It is 324 pages, 40 substantive recommendations. We spent a month in Alaska, combined time. We literally went from the east coast across the Country. We have been in Public Law 280 jurisdictions, where about half the Native people live and we have been in traditional Indian Country, as well. We never opened an office, we just worked in the fields.

And because we have the ground truth, we really had, I think, the means to do what you asked us to do. We have done it, which is to tell you in an unvarnished way what needs to be done, as best we could. We have done it unanimously.

I would just say a couple of things. One, Kevin Washburn I have known for many years. He is a fantastic public official, as is Tim Purdon and Brendan Johnson, as well, who was mentioned. The folks who serve are not the issue. The issue is a failed Federal system. The Indian Country system and the Public Law 280 system both are not producing the way they should. They will never be reformed, never, in a way that meets the needs of local communities as the way they should. Because in America, local justice is what we all trust. Having people self-govern, having people be able to vote in their own officials, to be transparent, accountable and accessible and to deal with the budget reality on the ground in a multi-year fashion, by the way, not subject to some annual appropriation from a distant place.

The dominant theme in this report is the failure of that system. And if you need any other example, post-traumatic stress disorder, the President talked about it, Congress has talked about it. The PTSD rate for returning vets from Afghanistan is the same as Native American juveniles in this Country. It is identical. One in four suffers from PTSD because they are so routinely exposed to violence in a way that is indefensible at this time and in this moment.

And we really can do something about these issues. We have a roadmap with recommendations that shows a transition point to local control, self-government. And the idea that we can protect every American's civil rights, which is key to this balance that we try to strike, we should be able to go through tribal courts and get to Federal courts to vindicate these rights.

But with that system, let these Indian nations choose. Let them choose whether they are Public Law 280 or whether they are a non-Public Law 280 State, to develop a system as we have outlined, with great specificity, included in our written testimony. You can adopt, let them choose for themselves and let them decide which laws work the best for their own communities and partner with the Federal Government or the States or both as they see fit and make it sovereign to sovereign. And the results will flow.

Wherever we saw reduced Federal control, reduced command and control, whether it is indirectly, through Public Law 280, or directly through U.S. Attorneys and the whole Federal justice system, well-intentioned through it may be, whenever tribes are free to do what they need to do, to set priorities and enforce their laws, with protection for civil rights, crime goes down. It is as simple as that. I don't know how else to say it except to say there is hope. But we have to change our thinking. And we should not be defending a system that is not working so well for people.

Finally, I would just say, it really is a privilege to be here. It is a privilege basically to work on these issues with you. We have sunset now, and you are gracious to keep us here for this hearing. If we can help you in the years to come, we will be glad to do it. I am very confident that within the next generation we will do the things in this roadmap. I have no doubt whatsoever. Because I know just from my own experience that these issues go beyond party lines. I want to thank Senator Reid for appointing me to this Commission. I was a George W. Bush U.S. Attorney, appointed by a President I dearly love and enjoyed serving and was honored to serve. There is no reason why we can't work together, as you have done so ably as Chair of this Committee, Madam Chair, to be able to do these things.

And finally, as a point of personal privilege, thank you for your letter about Washington's mascots. Much appreciated, on a personal level, by many of us who live in the field. Thank you.

[The joint prepared statement of Mr. Eid and Ms. Ellis follows:]

JOINT PREPARED STATEMENT OF TROY A. EID, CHAIRMAN, AND AFFIE ELLIS, COMMISSIONER, INDIAN LAW AND ORDER COMMISSION

Thank you for the opportunity to join you today. It is a privilege to discuss with you the Indian Law and Order Commission's November 2013 report, "A Roadmap for Making Native America Safer" (the "Roadmap"). The Roadmap can be downloaded at *www.indianlawandordercommission.com* or *http://www.aisc.ucla.edu/iloc/*.

Congress and the President created the Indian Law and Order Commission (the "Commission") by enacting the Tribal Law and Order Act of 2010 (TLOA). The Commission was charged by TLOA, and later the Violence Against Women Act Reauthorization Amendments of 2013 (VAWA Amendments), with assessing public safety challenges affecting all 566 federally recognized Indian tribes and nations. The Roadmap contains this assessment—perhaps the most comprehensive federal inquiry ever undertaken—and proposes reforms at the federal, state and tribal level to make Native American and Alaska Native communities safer and more just for all U.S. citizens.

While the Roadmap speaks for itself, a few points may stand out. First, the Roadmap's findings and recommendations are unanimous. They reflect the consensus views of all nine Commissioners, appointed by the President and Majority and Minority leadership of the Congress, Democrats and Republicans alike. The Commission's shared assessment and vision for safer Native American and Alaska Native nations attest to the bi-partisan—indeed, non-partisan—character of these very important issues.

Second, this report was written from the ground up. This Commission has operated entirely in the field for much of the past three years. We've done it without any permanent office, traveling from the East Coast to the outer reaches of Alaska, taking testimony and talking with thousands of people, Native and non-Native alike. The Roadmap's assessment, conclusions and proposals reflect the ground-truth of what we experienced across our great country. The practical realities of what works and what doesn't informed the Commission's endeavors at every stage. All nine commissioners vowed not to avoid the hard issues because we wanted to keep faith with the many inspirational people we met and learned from during this remarkable journey.

As this Committee well knows, American Indian and Alaska Native communities and lands are frequently less safe—and sometimes dramatically more dangerous—than most other places in our country. In short, the Commission found that throughout history, and continuing today, federal policies have displaced and diminished tribal institutions that are best positioned to provide trusted, accountable, accessible and cost-effective justice in Tribal communities.

In most U.S. communities, the Federal Government plays an important but limited role in criminal justice. State and local leaders have the authority and responsibility to address virtually all other public safety concerns. Precisely the opposite is true in much of Indian country. The Federal Government, and in some cases state governments, exercise substantial criminal jurisdiction on reservations. As a result,

Native people—including juveniles—frequently are caught up in a wholly nonlocal justice system. This system is complex, expensive, and simply cannot provide the criminal justice services that Native communities expect and deserve.

It is time for a change. The idea that local communities should and indeed must have jurisdiction to make and enforce their own criminal laws, if they so choose, is a bedrock principle of the American justice system. The federal courts can and will be accessible to criminal defendants, as a crucial part of the Roadmap's recommendations, if and when needed so that the federal civil rights of all U.S. citizens are fully protected.

Public safety in Indian country can improve dramatically once Native nations and Tribes have greater freedom to build and maintain their own criminal justice systems. The Commission sees breathtaking possibilities for safer, stronger Native communities achieved through home-grown, tribally based systems that respect the civil rights of all. The Commission rejects outmoded command-andcontrol policies, favoring increased local control, accountability, and transparency.

The Roadmap contains six chapters addressing: (1) Jurisdiction; (2) Reforming Justice for Alaska Natives; (3) Strengthening Tribal Justice; (4) Intergovernmental Cooperation; (5) Detention and Alternatives; and (6) Juvenile Justice. Throughout these chapters, the Roadmap offers 40 substantive proposals for making Native American and Alaska Native nations safer and more just, while protecting the civil rights of all U.S. citizens, Native and non-Native alike.

This Committee has approved important legislation in recent years to make Native America safer and more just. These reforms, including TLOA and the VAWA Amendments, are making a difference and we greatly appreciate your leadership. But much more can be done. We respectfully urge this Committee, the Congress and the President to put this Roadmap into action by implementing its recommendations as expeditiously as possible. These improvements will enable U.S. citizens to travel together from today's stubborn reality—where far too many Native American and Alaska Native communities suffer from violent crime—to a not-too-distant future where the public safety gap between Native America and the rest of the United States can finally be closed.

When the Commission first released the Roadmap last November, we were privileged to provide briefings to Members and professional staff from the Senate and the House, as well as The White House, U.S. Departments of Justice and the Interior, and other Executive Branch agencies. From these discussions emerged a request that the Commission provide even greater specificity as to how each of its 40 recommendations might be implemented—through legislation, Presidential executive order or Executive Branch policy directive, and so forth. The remainder of this testimony steps through the Roadmap to provide this supplemental information.

Again, and on behalf of the entire Commission, thank you for the privilege of serving. We appreciate your continued leadership and commitment to making Native America safer and more just.

Chapter 1: Jurisdiction

Congress

1. Enact a statute amending 18 and 25 U.S.C. so that any tribe subject to federal and/or state criminal jurisdiction under 18 U.S.C. §§ 1152, 1153, or 1162 will have the option to exclude itself from such jurisdiction, either fully or partially, and from the sentencing limits of the Indian Civil Rights Act, so long as it affords federal constitutional rights to defendants, and subject to limited review of such constitutional guarantees by an Article III court, the United States Court of Indian Appeals. Under this statute, tribes could also opt to return to federal and/or state jurisdiction. To the extent tribes exercise this option to exclude themselves from federal and/or state criminal jurisdiction, this law would also acknowledge tribal criminal jurisdiction over all individuals who commit offenses within Indian country.

2. Enact a statute establishing a new specialized Article III court, the United States Court of Indian Appeals, whose appellate jurisdiction would extend to cases arising in the courts of all tribes that have exercised the option to be excluded from federal and/or state criminal jurisdiction and from the sentencing limits of the Indian Civil Rights Act. The Court of Indian Appeals would be authorized to hear all appeals relating to alleged violations of the 4th, 5th, 6th, and 8th Amendments of the United States Constitution by such tribal courts, to interpret federal law related to criminal cases arising in federal [and possibly tribal] courts in Indian country, to hear and resolve federal questions involving the jurisdiction of tribal courts, and to address federal habeas corpus petitions from defendants in tribal courts, whether or not from tribes that have exercised the jurisdictional opt-out. In all cases of appeals from tribal courts to the Court of Indian Appeals, the defendant would be required to first exhaust tribal remedies. The law would make the Court of Indian

Appeals on the same level as the United States Circuit Courts of Appeal, and would authorize appeals from decisions of the Court of Indian Appeals to the United States Supreme Court, according to the current discretionary review process. Judges of the Court of Indian Appeals would be nominated by the President in consultation with tribes, and each panel of the Court would consist of at least three judges. The Court would have a permanent location within Indian country, and additional temporary locations throughout Indian country.

3. Amend the Speedy Trial Act, 18 U.S.C. § 1361, to apply to tribal courts to the extent they have opted out of federal and/or state jurisdiction.

4. Amend 25 U.S.C. § 1323 to authorize tribes subject to state criminal jurisdiction under 18 U.S.C. § 1162 or any other federal statute to retrocede that state jurisdiction back to the Federal Government.

Chapter 2: Alaska

Congress

1. Amend the Alaska Native Claims Settlement Act, 43 U.S.C. § 1601 et seq., to: (1) provide that former reservation lands acquired in fee by Alaska Native villages and other lands transferred in fee to Native villages pursuant to ANCSA are Indian country within the meaning of 18 U.S.C. § 1151, or, in the alternative, amend § 1151 to provide for a special Indian country designation for such lands; (2) clarify that Native allotments and Native-owned town sites in Alaska are Indian country within the meaning of the existing provisions of 18 U.S.C. § 1151; (3) clarify that the Secretary of Interior is authorized to take land into trust for Alaska tribes, including lands transferred to tribes from Regional Corporations or otherwise acquired by tribes in fee; 3) allow transfer of lands from Regional Corporations to tribal governments; (4) direct more resources to tribal governments for the provision of government services in those communities.

2. Repeal Section 910 of Title IX of the Violence Against Women Reauthorization Act of 2013 (VAWA Amendment), which excluded all Alaska tribes, except for the Metlakatla Indian Community, from other provisions of the Act which address tribal criminal jurisdiction and tribal protection orders.

3. Enact a statute affirming the inherent criminal jurisdiction of Alaska Native tribal governments over all Indians within the external boundaries of their villages.

Executive Branch

1. The Department of the Interior should amend 25 C.F.R. part 151 to eliminate the exception for Alaska and to provide a process and decisional criteria for the exercise of the Secretary's discretion to acquire land in trust for Alaska Natives.

2. The Secretary of the Interior should seek a legal opinion from the Solicitors' Office regarding the Indian country status of Alaska Native allotments and Alaska Native Townsites.

Chapter 3: Strengthening Tribal Justice

Congress

1. In accordance with existing studies and any additional studies as needed, appropriate funds sufficient to bring Indian country law enforcement coverage into parity with the United States, including tribes under state as well as federal criminal jurisdiction, tribes that do or do not compact for federal services under P.L. 93–638, and tribes that opt for exclusion from federal and/or state jurisdiction.

2. Enact a statute requiring state and local law enforcement agencies to report annually on criminal offenses occurring within the Indian country that is subject to their jurisdiction through federal authorization.

3. Enact a statute requiring the United States Department of Justice to provide reservation-level victimization data from its annual crime victimization surveys. 4. Amend the Tribal Law and Order Act of 2010 to allow tribes to sue the Departments of Justice and Interior if they fail to produce and submit annual Indian country crime data and reports as required by the Act.

5. Amend 18 U.S.C. § 3006A to direct each federal district court whose district encompasses Indian country, in developing its plan for indigent defense, to include a program for the appointment of qualified tribal public defenders as special assistant public defenders in Indian country cases, similar to the program established under 18 U.S.C. § 2810(d) for the appointment of Special Assistant United States Attorneys.

6. Enact a statute encouraging United States District Courts that hear Indian country cases to hold more judicial proceedings and provide more judicial services (e.g., probation) in and near Indian country.

7. Commission the Congressional Research Service to study the value and desirability of expanding the current pool of United States Magistrates in order to improve criminal justice access and services to Indian country.

8. Enact a statute similar to the Transfer Act for Indian Health Services, P.L. 83–568, Aug. 5, 1954, transferring all of the functions, responsibilities, duties, and authorities of the Department of the Interior relating to the provision of law enforcement and justice services to Indian country, as set forth in 25 U.S.C. § 2802, to the Department of Justice, and consolidating them with existing services and programs for Indian country within DOJ. The law would establish a new Indian country entity within the Department of Justice, headed by an Assistant Attorney General, to house the new consolidated services and programs, including an appropriate number of FBI agents and their support resources. The statute should specify that Indian preference, as set forth in 25 U.S.C. § 472, applies to positions in the Department of Justice carrying out the transferred functions, and that the new entity exercises the trust responsibility of the United States toward Indian nations. It should also specify that the provisions of the Indian Self-Determination and Education Assistance Act, 25 U.S.C. § 450 et seq., addressing contracts with tribes for federal services and Self-Governance agreements apply to the Department of Justice in carrying out its law enforcement and justice services for Indian country. The statute would direct cost savings from the consolidation to the new Indian country entity, and maintain at least that level of funding over time.

9. Enact a statute ending all grant-based, competitive Indian country criminal justice funding in DOJ, and pool the funds to establish a permanent, recurring base funding system for tribal law enforcement and justice services, administered by the new Indian country entity within DOJ. This base funding would be available on an equal basis to all tribes choosing to provide law enforcement and/or justice services, including tribes under state as well as federal criminal jurisdiction, tribes that do or do not compact for federal services under P.L. 93–638, and tribes that opt for exclusion from federal and/or state jurisdiction. The statute would also authorize DOJ to set aside 5 percent of the consolidated grant monies each year as a tribal criminal justice system capacity-building fund. Under the statute, the formula for distributing base funding and a method for awarding capacity-building dollars would be developed by DOJ in consultation with tribes.

10. Enact the funding requests for Indian country public safety in the National Congress of American Indians Indian Country Budget Request for FY 2014, and consolidate these funds within the new Indian country entity in DOJ. These requests include full funding of all provisions in the Tribal Law and Order Act of 2010, funding of the Indian Tribal Justice Act of 1993 ($50 million/year for seven years for tribal court base funding) and a 7 percent Indian country set-aside from all Office of Justice Programs.

11. Fund the Legal Services Corporation (LSC) at a level that will allow LSC to provide the public defense services in tribal court that it was authorized to provide under the Tribal Law and Order Act of 2010. Such appropriated funds shall be provided directly to tribal governments so tribes may have flexibility to provide criminal defense services separately, if they so choose, from existing civil legal aid agencies and organizations.

Executive Branch

1. In accordance with existing studies and any additional studies as needed, recommend appropriation of funds sufficient to bring Indian country law enforcement coverage into parity with the United States, including tribes under state as well as federal criminal jurisdiction, tribes that do or do not compact for federal services under P.L. 93–638, and tribes that opt for exclusion from federal and/or state jurisdiction.

2. The FBI should revise its NIBRS uniform incident reporting system to establish "Indian country" (or not) as a separate category within "Offense," apart from "Location" characteristics.

3. The United States Department of Justice, Bureau of Justice Statistics, should extract and report annual victimization data at the reservation level in its National Crime Victimization Survey.

4. The Attorney General should issue a directive affirming that federally deputized tribal prosecutors appointed as Special Assistant United States Attorneys pursuant to 25 U.S.C. § 2810(d) are entitled to all Law Enforcement Sensitive information needed to perform their jobs for their tribes. The United States Attorneys Manual and all training programs and manuals provided to the FBI and other federal law enforcement agencies should be updated to incorporate this directive.

5. The Attorney General should issue a directive creating a presumption that federal officials shall serve as witnesses in tribal court proceedings when subpoenaed

by tribal courts to do so, and streamline the process for granting permission to such officials to testify when subpoenaed or otherwise directed by tribal court judges.

Chapter 4: Intergovernmental Cooperation

Congress

1. Appropriate funds to support training costs and other requirements for tribes seeking to have their agencies and officers certified by state POST agencies for purposes of exercising state peace officer powers.

2. Enact a statute creating a federally subsidized insurance pool or similarly affordable arrangement for tort liability for tribes seeking to enter into a deputization agreement with state and/or local law enforcement agencies.

3. Amend the Federal Tort Claims Act, 28 U.S.C. § 1346(b), to include unequivocal coverage for tribal police, coverage that is not contingent on the exercise of discretion by U.S. Attorneys or other federal officials.

4. Enact a statute requiring state authorities to notify the relevant tribal government when they have reason to believe that they have arrested a tribal citizen who resides in Indian country, and when they have reason to believe that a tribal citizen who resides in Indian country is a criminal defendant in a state proceeding. When a tribal citizen is a defendant in a state proceeding, the relevant tribe should be notified at all steps of the process, be invited to have representatives present at any hearing, and be invited to collaborate in choices involving corrections placement or community supervision. These obligations would be contingent on the arrestee/defendant providing his/her consent and the tribe informing state authorities of the appropriate point of contact with the tribe.

5. Enact a statute providing Byrne grants or COPS grants for data-sharing ventures to local and state governments, conditioned on the state or local governments entering into agreements to provide criminal offenders' history records to any tribe with an operating law enforcement agency that requests data sharing. State and local governments that did not make such agreements would be ineligible for Byrne and COPS grants.

Executive Branch

1. The Department of Justice should establish a model tribal-state law enforcement agreement program, to help states formulate uniform laws to enable MOUs and agreements with tribes, both in states that have jurisdiction under Public Law 280 or similar laws and in states that do not have such federallyauthorized criminal jurisdiction.

2. The Departments of Justice and Interior should require their law enforcement officers to notify the relevant tribal governing when they arrest a tribal citizen who resides in Indian country and when a citizen who resides in Indian country is a criminal defendant in a federal court proceeding, including the outcome of that proceeding. The United States Probation Department should establish a policy that when a tribal citizen has been convicted in a federal proceeding for an offense committed within Indian country, it will notify the relevant tribal government and invite that tribe to collaborate in choices involving corrections placement or community supervision.

3. The Departments of Justice and Interior should establish policies of providing written notice to the relevant tribal governing body regarding any tribal citizens who are reentering tribal lands from jail or prison or who are being released from jail or prison on tribal lands, whether or not that citizen formerly resided on the reservation. These obligations would be contingent on the tribe informing federal authorities of the appropriate point of contact with the tribal governing body.

Chapter 5: Detention and Alternatives

Congress

1. All appropriations for reentry, second-chance, and alternatives to incarceration (funding, technical assistance, training, etc.) should include a commensurate amount set aside for Indian country. These funds should be managed by the new Indian country entity within DOJ and administered using a permanent, recurring base funding system. This base funding would be available on an equal basis to all tribes exercising criminal jurisdiction, including tribes under state as well as federal criminal jurisdiction, tribes that do or do not compact for federal services under P.L. 93–638, and tribes that opt for exclusion from federal and/or state jurisdiction. Under the statute, the formula for distributing base funding and a method for awarding capacity-building dollars would be developed by DOJ in consultation with tribes.

2. All appropriations for construction, operation, and maintenance of jails, prisons, and other corrections programs should include a commensurate amount set aside for Indian country. Those funds, together with funds for existing programs for offenders

convicted under tribal law, should be consolidated and administered by the Indian country entity within the Department of Justice.

3. Appropriate funds that supply incentives for development of high-quality regional Indian country detention facilities, capable of housing offenders in need of higher security and providing rehabilitative programming beyond "warehousing."

4. Convert the Bureau of Prisons pilot program created by the Tribal Law and Order Act into a permanent programmatic option that tribes can use to house prisoners.

Executive Branch

In budget requests, prioritize incentives for development of high-quality regional Indian country detention facilities, capable of housing offenders in need of higher security and providing rehabilitative programming beyond "warehousing."

Chapter 6: Juvenile Justice

Congress

1. Amend 18 and 25 U.S.C. so that any tribe subject to federal and/or state juvenile jurisdiction under 18 U.S.C. §§ 1152, 1153, or 1162 will have the option to exclude itself from such jurisdiction and from the sentencing limits of the Indian Civil Rights Act, so long as it affords federal constitutional rights to juveniles, and subject to limited review of such constitutional guarantees by an Article III court, the United States Court of Indian Appeals.

2. Amend the Federal Delinquency Act, 18 U.S.C. § 5032, to add "or tribe" after the word "state" in subsections (1) and (2). The effect will be that federal prosecution may not proceed against a juvenile for any offense under 18 U.S.C. §§ 1152 and 1153 unless the prosecutor certifies, after investigation, that at least one of the following three conditions exists: (1) the Tribe does not have jurisdiction or refuses to assume jurisdiction over the juvenile; (2) the Tribe does not have programs or services available and adequate for the needs of juveniles; or 3) the offense is a violent felony or a specified drug offense in which there is a "substantial federal interest."

3. Amend the Federal Delinquency Act, 18 U.S.C. § 5032, to provide: "Notwithstanding §§ 1152 and 1153, no person subject to the criminal jurisdiction of an Indian tribal government for any offense the Federal jurisdiction for which is predicated solely on Indian country (as defined in § 1151), and which has occurred within the boundaries of such Indian country, shall be proceeded against as an adult unless the governing body of the Tribe has elected that federal law providing for transfer of juvenile cases for criminal prosecution shall have effect over land and persons subject to its criminal jurisdiction."

4. Amend the definition of "child custody proceeding" in the Indian Child Welfare Act, 25 U.S.C. § 1903(1), to delete the following language: "Such term or terms shall not include a placement based upon an act which, if committed by an adult, would be deemed a crime . . .." The effect will be that in some juvenile proceedings involving such acts (mainly those where the child resides or is domiciled in Indian country) tribal jurisdiction will be exclusive of the state, and in other such proceedings there will be a presumption in favor of transferring the matter from state to tribal court.

5. Enact a statute similar to the transfer act for Indian health services, P.L. 83-568, Aug. 5, 1954, transferring all of the functions, responsibilities, duties, and authorities of the Department of the Interior relating to the provision of juvenile justice services to Indian country, as set forth in 25 U.S.C. § 2802 and otherwise, to the Department of Justice.

6. Enact a statute modeled on the Indian Child Welfare Act, 25 U.S.C. § 1901 et seq., providing that in every Federal and State juvenile proceeding where the court has reason to believe the juvenile is an "Indian child" as defined in 25 U.S.C. § 1903(4), the state or federal court must seek verification of the juvenile's status from either the BIA or the juvenile's Tribe in accordance with BIA Guidelines for State Courts: Indian Child Custody Proceedings, November 26, 1979, 44 Fed. Reg. 67584, § B.1; must notify the juvenile's Tribe in the manner provided in 25 U.S.C. § 1912; and must afford the juvenile's Tribe the right to intervene as specified in 25 U.S.C. § 1911(c). This statute should also include a requirement that state and federal courts exercising jurisdiction over "Indian children" for acts occurring in Indian country maintain records at every stage of the proceedings, including detention, noting the status of the juvenile as an "Indian child" and the juvenile's tribal affiliation(s).

7. Enact a statute, modeled on Section 712 of the U.S. Attorneys' Manual, directing federal courts to establish a pre-trial diversion program for Indian country juvenile cases that utilizes the tribal probation department of any participating tribe as

the agency responsible for establishing a pre-trial diversion agreement and certifying compliance with that agreement.

8. Enact a statute providing that when an Indian juvenile is detained for treatment pursuant to state or federal court order for acts carried out in Indian country, the detaining agency must ensure that the treatment is informed by the most recent and best trauma research as applied to Indian country, as certified by the Department of Justice, and, consistent with provision of such treatment, is provided in a facility that is community-based or located within a reasonable distance from the juvenile's home.

Executive Branch

1. The Department of Justice, in consultation with tribal representatives, shall establish standards for treatment of Indian juveniles that is informed by the most recent trauma research as applied to Indian country.

2. Regulations governing federal law enforcement, probation, and prosecution agencies should be modified to ensure that at the time Indian juveniles are brought before federal juvenile justice agencies, those juveniles are provided with trauma-informed screening and care, carried out in consultation with tribal child welfare and behavioral health agencies.

3. The cost to the Federal Government of federal and state Indian country juvenile jurisdiction should be determined, and whenever a Tribe opts out of federal and/or state jurisdiction, the federal funds that would otherwise go to federal and/or state agencies should instead be directed to the Tribe.

4. Consolidate Department of Justice funding for Indian country juvenile justice as block funding rather than as grants, affording tribes the option to direct funds to treatment rather than detention.

5. In budget requests, funding levels for tribal juvenile justice should be established at a level of parity with state juvenile justice for every tribe exercising juvenile jurisdiction.

Conclusion

Again, the members of the Commission are committed to continuing to work with this Committee and the Congress to support the effective implementation of the recommendations contained in our Roadmap. The Roadmap reflects the unanimous bipartisan consensus for how justice can be strengthened to benefit the lives of all people living and working in Native American and Alaska Native nations across our country. We look forward to supporting your continued efforts to make Native American and Alaska Native communities safer and more just for all U.S. citizens.

The CHAIRWOMAN. Thank you. Thank you for that.

Ms. Truett Jerue, nice to see you here in Washington. Thank you very much, and you are welcome to provide your testimony.

STATEMENT OF TAMI TRUETT JERUE, DIRECTOR OF SOCIAL SERVICES/TRIBAL ADMINISTRATOR, ANVIK TRIBAL COUNCIL

Ms. JERUE. I am not used to speaking like this, but I appreciate being here. I am very honored to have been asked, Madam Chair, and to the honored Senators, Senator Begich and Senator Murkowski, both for which I have a great deal of respect.

I know that testimony was submitted for me, with some of my thoughts in it. But I think that I really wanted to speak to you, and I think that I was asked to speak to you as a Native woman. I am not a lawyer, I am an advocate. I live in a very small, remote, isolated community, in Anvik, Alaska, on the Yukon River. I flew out on Monday morning at 10:30 on 40 mile winds on a 207 and I was thinking, where is the snow?

[Laughter.]

Ms. TRUETT JERUE. So I really do want to clarify a few points. The main things that I really want to talk to you about is, I live in Anvik, my family lives in Anvik. I worry day to day about the regular things that we worry about as parents and going to work and the things that we need, oil in the stove. But I also worry about whether my children, my nieces, nephews, or relatives are going to be hurt today. And in Anvik, I consider us a fairly safe community.

But I would like to, when I have to have a conversation with my 14 year old son, when he gets out his snow machine and goes to school in the morning, hey, I want you to come home early today, the booze came in on the plane, I don't want you to be out there, because I am afraid that the drunks are going to be, I am afraid for you, not because of you, but the other people that are drinking. Or when I have to tell my 18 year old niece who I know is going to be drinking, even though I know she shouldn't be, that she needs to be careful about who hands her that drink, and where she is, and to be aware, those are the things that I have to worry about every day.

Or if I get a phone call, who is calling me. Is it because I am going to have a callout to go respond to domestic violence? Am I going to get a callout so I have to go bring some kids for the night? I do that all the time, not as part of my job, but as part of my community.

I am married to a chief of the community. He has been Chief for about 23 years. That doesn't give me any special privileges, in fact, I think it not a good thing sometimes.

[Laughter.]

Ms. TRUETT JERUE. But what I really want to make very clear here is this is reality. The report is an amazing report. I am so honored to sit here with you all. We got to be heard. And I don't know when that really has happened.

After having read this report, I want to really be clear, though, Alaska, we have all these dangerous realities in our lives. And there are a lot of reasons why, and you stated it very clearly in your report about that. But we are not victims. We are not victims. We may have been victimized, and we may have been victimized by the system and we may be victimized even in our own communities.

But we are not sitting here as victims. We are strong, Native people. We have a right to live where we live. We have a right to command that we have safety. We have a right to command the same types of daily protections that you all have. I can't get on there and say 9–1–1, and get somebody to come and help me. It may take me two or three days to get resources. But there are people I can call. There are safe places that will help me. There are places that I can go.

So I want to be really clear in this. And I know there are several other things that I should say, but I really want to speak for the women, the children, the men who have been victimized, who have worked so hard to not live as victims. But also, I really, really encourage the work that we have done over the last 30 years in domestic violence, we have done some amazing things. We do need to amend 910, we do need to do that in VAWA 2013. That has to happen. It is just one of those basic protections that we can utilize as communities to help our own people. That is the message that I really want to leave with you. I have so many stories, it would take months.

Thank you, and I am really honored to be in this room with you all, and your allowing me to talk with you about this.

[The prepared statement of Ms. Truett Jerue follows:]

PREPARED STATEMENT OF TAMI TRUETT JERUE, DIRECTOR OF SOCIAL SERVICES/ TRIBAL ADMINISTRATOR, ANVIK TRIBAL COUNCIL

Chairman Tester, Vice-Chairman Barrasso and distinguished Members of the Committee, thank you for holding today's hearing on the Indian Law and Order report. I would also like to personally thank the Commission for its hard work and commitment to Alaska. My name is Tami Truett Jerue and I am from the village of Anvik, an Athabascan village located on the Yukon River in Western Interior Alaska. Anvik is a small Deg Hit'an Athabascan community with a very rich history. We are located on the west bank of the Yukon River in Interior Alaska, just inside the old mouth of the Anvik River along the hillside. We are a very isolated, federally recognized Tribe with 275 enrolled citizens, for whom we have responsibility to protect and serve. We are not on the State's road system and we travel in and out of the village by air, boat, or snow machine.

I am honored to also speak for the 37 federally recognized tribes that make up the Tanana Chiefs Conference, an inter-tribal health and social services consortium that serves an area of Interior Alaska that is almost the size of Texas, and I bring the message of over 200 tribes across Alaska.

As a life-long village resident and tribal social services director, with 30 years of professional experience in tribal child protection, domestic violence, sexual assault, substance abuse and therapeutic counseling, I assure you that the Law and Order Commission Report's chapter dedicated to Alaska is no exaggeration, and that the statistics, data, quotes and findings in the 23 page chapter only briefly touch on the social ills that Alaska Natives confront and seek to change. Everything you have read in this Report about levels of violence and assault in our Alaska Native communities is absolutely true. We have the most severe rates of domestic violence and sexual assault compared to any other communities in the United States. Yet as tribal governments, the crippling legal structure crafted by Congress and the State of Alaska have severely compromised our ability to do anything more to heal and protect our people.

We agree with the Commission's statement that "ANCSA got Indian policy in Alaska wrong." To be sure, ANCSA was well-intentioned, and we applaud the efforts of the many ANSCA corporations' boards and staff that carry-out well the missions of their various companies. ANCSA corporations have certainly had positive impacts on the Alaskan economy. At the same time, because of ANCSA and the flawed interpretations of ANCSA by the Supreme Court and by the State of Alaska, Alaska Tribes today are denied the most basic of governmental tools necessary to exercise true local self-government and to reverse the alarming and tragic rates of violence, substance abuse and suicide. It is Congress's duty to fix this flawed structure, and to reverse and discontinue the practice of exempting Alaska Tribes from national policies and programs that are available to Tribes everywhere else; our tribal children and communities, our women, will all continue to suffer if nothing is done.

I ask that you seriously consider carrying out all the Commission's recommendations. For today, let me just discuss a few of them.

First, Alaska tribes need a land base to provide public safety, quality education, natural resource management, and economic opportunity for our tribal citizens. This land base can be created by two means: first, by clarifying land status; and second, by giving Alaska Tribes the option to have their lands placed into trust. Finally, to protect Alaska Native women it is essential that Section 910 of VAWA be repealed, as TCC President Isaac requested in his recent testimony on S. 919 (a bill to amend Title IV of the Indian Self-Determination Act, and for other purposes).

The Indian Country Status of Townsites and Allotments Must Be Clarified

An immediate step this Committee can take to provide a land base to Tribes in Alaska is to confirm the Indian Country status of the approximately 6 million acres of individual Native allotments and communal village townsites located throughout the state. These lands, presently held in restricted fee status and not related to ANCSA, already satisfy the "federal supremacy" requirement for Indian Country described by the Supreme Court in the Venetie decision. Furthermore, their prevalence in scores of Villages across Alaska already provides many tribal governments with an existing land base upon which to exercise authority.

The Interior Department has been reluctant to affirm the legal status of these lands through regulation, adjudication or the issuance of a firm legal opinion. By providing minor alterations to the definition of Indian Country, this Committee is uniquely situated to bring clarity to this long-unsettled issue. I respectfully urge this Committee to enact legislation confirming that Alaska Tribes (1) have an existing land base in the form of townsite and allotment lands, and that (2) that land base enjoys the same legal Indian Country status as exists for Indian lands in the lower 48 States.

Alaska Tribes Should Be Able to Have Their Land Taken Into Federal Trust Status

Tribes in Alaska, like all other federally-recognized Tribes, exercise and enjoy a government-to-government relationship with the United States. But when it comes to trust lands, we have again been treated differently from other Tribes in the United States. Until recently, Alaska's Tribes were prohibited from petitioning the Secretary of the Interior to place our lands into trust status under Section 5 of the Indian Reorganization Act. Although the trust lands issue is presently in litigation, and despite a victory for our Tribes, I want to emphasize to this Committee that the present federal policy remains one of prohibition: Alaska's tribes are still denied the right to have our lands placed into trust status.

What our communities seek is choice; we seek the right to decide for ourselves whether trust lands status is in the best interests of our Tribes and our tribal communities. Some Tribes may conclude that it is in their best interest to have local lands be in ANCSA corporate ownership. Others may conclude it is in their best interest to have their tribal lands be in fee simple ownership. But some will decide it is in their best interests to have their lands protected through federal trust status, and that choice should be ours, alone, to make. This is the heart of tribal self-determination and self-governance. Tribes in Alaska deserve the opportunity to maximize their self-determination just as much as any other Tribes in America.

Placing land-into-trust would enhance the ability of our Tribes to provide public safety and related services to village residents, concurrent with the State of Alaska. Many of our Tribes are ready and able to take on such public services with some adjustments to local tribal ordinances, and codes, and with existing funding available through federal agencies like the Bureau of Indian Affairs and the Department of Justice. In the Interior region of Alaska, most of our Tribes have active tribal courts, but current funding constraints and narrow jurisdiction limit our opportunities to heal our people, address drug and alcohol issues, and protect our women and children from domestic violence.

Section 910 of VAWA Must Be Repealed

Section 910 of the recently reauthorized Violence Against Woman Act (VAWA) prevents 228 Alaska Tribes and their tribal courts from being able to adequately address domestic and sexual violence in our communities. This Alaska Exception is one of many such unwarranted exceptions that have treated Tribes in Alaska differently from Tribes in the Lower 48. Given our extraordinarily high numbers of domestic violence and sexual assault, Section 910 only further endangers our communities. This measure is ethically repugnant and must be repealed at once. Last month, Tanana Chiefs Conference President Jerry Isaac encouraged this Committee to repeal Section 910 at once as it considers Senate Bill 919. I join President Isaac in respectfully encouraging you to add a provision to S. 919 repealing section 910 of VAWA and to mark-up and pass S. 919 as swiftly as possible. As President Isaac so eloquently said: "Our women cannot wait. Our Children cannot wait." The time to act is *now*.

The Alaska Safe Families and Villages Act (S. 1474) Should Be Amended and Swiftly Enacted Into Law

Finally, I respectfully request that this Committee consider and amend S. 1474, the proposed Alaska Safe Families and Villages Act. S. 1474's current provisions should be merged with S. 1192, which was considered in the 112th Congress. It is absolutely essential that, without regard to technical land titles and the technical "Indian country" status of lands or tribal communities, *our Tribes must have the tools necessary to combat drug and alcohol abuse, domestic violence, and violence against women*. Fighting these scourges in our communities and healing our people cannot be made to stand on technicalities. We need to get to work, and *now*. And we need Congress's help to do that. The State is not the problem, because the State is nowhere to be found in most of our Villages. It is our sacred responsibility to protect our people, and Congress has an equally sacred obligation to our Tribes, to our women and to our children, to enact a bill that will, once and for all, secure to our Tribes the tools necessary to do so. Please amend and pass the Alaska Safe Families and Villages Act. Today, the Tribes of Alaska come to you, not as victims of a failed governmental policy, but as powerful and responsible advocates for our people. We are stepping up to do what we must do. But without equally firm action from Congress, our people will suffer, we will continue with decades more of litigation battles, and loopholes will continue to be found which deny our Tribes the funding necessary to improve law and order in our communities. Our tribal courts will continue their work as best they can—they have courage and commitment I cannot begin to convey here today—but they will remain handicapped and our communities will continue to suffer. Real, lasting, positive change will escape us.

As you consider the Law and Order Commission's Report and Recommendations, please consider my story, my extended family, and my small but precious community. To me, the statistics revealed in this Report tell the story of real people who I love and care for. They deserve better. Please equip our Tribes with the practical and effective tools we need to heal ourselves. If Congress does its part, we will do ours.

Thank you for the opportunity to testify today on the Commission's historical report. And many thanks to the incredibly brave women from our Tribes who shared their personal and horrific stories with the Commission. They are silent no more, and your hearing today honors them more than anyone.

The CHAIRWOMAN. Thank you. Thank you very much for traveling all this way to be here, and for your passion on these issues.

Ms. Ellis, I am going to start with you. You talked about the structural issue between DOI and Justice and appropriating funds. To me it is something we should look at pursuing. We had a similar issue between Hanford, injured worker issues in the Department of Energy and Department of License. It doesn't mean that both people are involved, it is just, which is the better agency for actually administering the program.

And in this case, I think what I heard you say, what I would like you to expound on, you are saying that DOI isn't responding fast enough or doesn't have the law enforcement experience to determine how to allocate those resources. So you are saying it is better done through the Department of Justice?

Ms. ELLIS. Madam Chair, thank you so much for the question. I also want to thank you for letting us have Theresa Pouley serve on our commission. She did a wonderful job representing the State of Washington. And particularly the Tulalip Tribe. When we talk about bright spots in Indian Country, Tulalip is certainly one of those areas.

I would not say though that the law enforcement personnel or services that are housed in the BIA are doing necessarily a bad job. I think it is more of a situation where you have the left hand doing something and the right hand is not—I think I am getting this mixed up too, as I am trying to illustrate with my hands. They are not talking to each other. And when you look at the difference between the Department of Interior, which houses other agencies, such as the National Park Service and the Bureau of Land Management, versus the Department of Justice with its specific focus on reducing crime in the Country, the Commission believes that the Department of Justice is better suited to handle more of the law enforcement needs, rather than the Department of Interior.

The CHAIRWOMAN. That would be like a grant program, to have the expertise to make the decisions where the funding should go? What specifically?

Ms. ELLIS. We are looking at efficiencies and trying to find ways for government to be more efficient. We keep pointing to the move of Indian Health Service no longer being housed within the Department of Interior but being transferred over to the Department of Health and Human Services. So that is the kind of situation that we are talking about, is transferring the current duties that are being performed within the BIA, Department of Interior house being transferred over to Department of Justice.

The CHAIRWOMAN. I think Mr. Purdon and Mr. Eid both, to me it is building on that expertise, and if you want it to work together, then having Indian Country and the Department of Justice work together more is like building infrastructure capacity. I don't know whether you have any more comments about that, Mr. Eid?

Mr. EID. Yes, I do. When I was U.S. Attorney in Colorado, it was typical. I served for a little bit more than three years. More than half the time I was there, the detention center the BIA had in our district was not funded, even though DOJ had built it with capital grants. So it sat empty. We sent our detainees up to South Dakota, typically. And sometimes farther away.

The prosecutor that BIA had to provide was not funded for 14 months of that, and there was no public defender for four years. It wasn't funded. So we had a completely dysfunctional justice system for almost five years. I happened to serve during most of that time. It is typical that the right hand, which is Interior, does not know what the left hand, which is Justice, is doing. They need to be consolidated in one place. We think DOJ is where the law enforcement functions should go, it should all go to DOJ, including all the law enforcement folks that serve in the Office of Justice Services. They need to go into the Department of Justice, they can be managed by an Assistant Attorney General and be accountable on one place to this Committee and to the rest of the Congress.

The CHAIRWOMAN. Thank you. Vice Chairman Barrasso?

Senator BARRASSO. Thank you very much, Madam Chairwoman.

Ms. Ellis, just thinking about what Ivan Posey, council member for the Eastern Shoshone Tribe, has been working on, you talked about stronger preventive services, suicide prevention, that all these services be provided for our Indian youth. Then these services will serve to reduce the unacceptably high numbers of Native youth entering the justice system.

I am just wondering how you think preventive services are going to assist in reducing the number of Indian youth in the justice system.

Mr. ELLIS. Thank you so much, Senator Barrasso, Mr. Vice Chairman. Our report talks about some of the programs that are existing at Wind River. Some of them have been award-winning. But again, back to my point about grant-based funding, too often you get a great program up and running, it runs out of money, and then it ceases to exist until another grant opportunity arises. We heard that at Wind River and we heard that across the Country with people we talked to.

One thing that our report emphasizes, though, is there are some solutions that just need to be community-driven, driven by tribes and organizations. I think Councilman Posey's testimony speaks to that. He talks about things that he is working on, and efforts that the Eastern Shoshone and Northern Arapaho Tribes are trying to tackle on a reservation basis.

So to the extent that the Federal Government and State governments can support those efforts, we think it is important that ultimately, those need to be community-driven.

Senator BARRASSO. In your testimony, you talked about some of the things you heard as you traveled were that people locally said things that we did, rather than what the government did. One of the highlights the Commission points to in the report is a lack of Federal judges and Federal courthouses. You made the point about how there was money to build a courthouse but not money to staff them, just some amazing inconsistencies of a bureaucracy. I am wondering about the barriers for criminal justice in Indian Country, specifically relating to Federal judges, courthouses. Our U.S. Attorney for Wyoming, Kip Crofts, also shared that view in his written testimony submitted to the Commission.

Ms. Ellis, can you talk about how you think this lack of Federal judges and courthouses affects Wind River Reservation?

Ms. ELLIS. Thank you again for that question, Vice Chairman. In Wyoming, as you know, and everybody in this room is very familiar with it, you come from large States with large land bases, and you are in the car for hours and hours driving, just to get from one town to another. That scenario becomes particularly difficult when you are talking about a place like Wind River where I think it is about a three and a half or four hour drive from the Wind River Reservation to Cheyenne, Wyoming, where the Article 3 judges are housed.

U.S. Attorney Kip Crofts in Wyoming has suggested that we start moving more of these court proceedings closer to Indian Country. Our report discusses perhaps using some magistrate judges in various roles to help ease the burden on some of these court functions. We also talk about a situation where Federal court proceedings have actually been held, criminal court proceedings held in Indian Country. I am proud to say that the Navajo Nation has been one of those areas.

So we think that it just makes sense. We didn't do any empirical data saying, it will save you this much money if you move a court proceeding closer to Indian Country, but we think it makes sense. And in the long run, it adds a little bit more to the institutional legitimacy, as people are able to go to these trials, hear what these people did, understand what happened in the courtroom. Right now, that is very foreign. People don't have the resources on reservations to travel to Cheyenne, for example, to see what is going on down there. So it is a bit of a mystery, and I think it would just help increase the transparency of what happens in these proceedings when we move them closer to Indian Country.

Senator BARRASSO. Mr. Chairman, anything you would like to add to that in terms of what you have seen across the spectrum?

Mr. EID. I appreciate it very much, Mr. Vice Chairman.

My State of Colorado, we have two Indian nations, they are 400 miles and 360 miles, respectively, from the nearest U.S. District courthouse. In the entire 20th century, there was exactly one U.S. District Court tribal in Indian Country, one. It was in 2005, in Shiprock, on the Navajo Nation, Chief Judge Vasquez presided in a murder case.

Part of the issue is just having the access that is local. So why we took this next step with the structural reform is we want to have a world where tribes who are ready and willing to accept the consequences can opt out of Federal jurisdiction, except for laws of general application. For example, in my State, the Southern Ute Indian Tribe, it is such a great tribe and such a great justice system that the Federal Government already contracts to put the Federal detainees, in the U.S. Attorneys office cases, they go to the jail at Southern Ute. They don't go to LaPlata County or the surrounding counties. They go the tribal jail, because it is a better jail. And it is better.

And so a tribe like that could assert that jurisdiction now if they provide the civil rights on the back end, let them opt out of the Federal justice system. They have their own laws, they can enforce them for just about anything that happens down there. If they are not ready, they don't have to do it. If they don't choose to do it, that is fine. But I think that will also help this judicial access issue, because I am pretty sure that Congress is not going to be able to find funds to build another whole round of Federal courthouses in distant places. We have to find a way that is easier for people to do.

Finally, as Commissioner Ellis said, magistrates can really help, I know, on a lot of these dockets. They can be a very valuable way to support judges. And then judges getting out in the field as well is another way. There is no plan right now in the judicial conference to do this. But there should be one plan, and I think it is appropriate in their oversight that there be a plan. They can decide what the plan is, but they should be able to account to you for what that plan is.

Senator BARRASSO. Thank you.

Thank you, Madam Chairwoman.

The CHAIRWOMAN. Thank you. Senator Heitkamp?

Senator HEITKAMP. Thank you again.

A couple quick questions. Mr. Eid, I am encouraged by your talking about MOUs and cooperative agreements. But I have to tell you, I have tried to negotiate them. I think we can all agree that when everybody works together and when we provide a collective network, so that jurisdictional differences or jurisdictional boundaries do not prevent justice from being served, that is the better method.

But there is one element here, and that is called trust. And it gets in the way every time you go, and try, trust me, I am a veteran of trying to negotiate these kinds of agreements. In your discussions on the Commission, can you tell me how or whether you considered this trust issue as you deliberated and came to this conclusion?

Mr. EID. Senator, I really appreciate that question. I must tell you that we have many robust debates. Can you force States to do these things? I was a State cabinet officer in Colorado for five years. I think the answer is no, you can't force the States to do it. But what you can do is make it easier for them in a practical way. You can have, for example, a risk pool for insurance that makes it possible so that everyone who participates in a task force or is involved in some sort of interagency agreement can be insured. That is one of the recommendations we have in this report.

You can also amend laws like the Federal Tort Claims Act which this Committee could do, to make it clear that if a tribal or State officer is operating as a Federal agent under existing law to enforce Federal laws, such as in a domestic violence case, they are insured and the government will stand behind. With all due respect, it is not up to some U.S. Attorney to say that they don't get insured.

Senator HEITKAMP. Let's flip that around, because you are talking about State impediments. Obviously I was a State official trying to make that happen.

Mr. EID. Yes.

Senator HEITKAMP. My resistance really came from tribal authorities.

Mr. EID. With all due respect, I think that when you stick your neck out like you did, and you can put those steps forward in the Federal system and in the State systems, the tribes will begin to reciprocate. I think until we do that, it is much harder to gain the trust, frankly, because you have the ability to point to something and say look, we will insure you, but this is what we expect out of you in return.

Senator HEITKAMP. I don't want to belabor the point. But I think it is significant, given the importance you put to this issue, and that is that until people believe that tribal, State and Federal authorities will act in unison and without bias, it is going to be extraordinarily difficult to do that kind of agreement.

Mr. EID. I agree.

Senator HEITKAMP. Because right away, it is, I do not want the county sheriff having that jurisdiction on that State road. And I can give you examples where I tried to get DUI convictions from tribal courts so that we could handle the licensure, a bus driver at over .2 who the tribal court would not give me their conviction for driving under the influence so we could revoke a bus driver's license.

So these are very complicated and historically very difficult issues. I think as we go forward in implementing these, we need to take the steps that we took in VAWA to build the trust, to build the relationship, to work collaboratively. This isn't something that can happen tomorrow, I guess is my point. I do want to talk a little bit about juveniles, because I think that if we looked at the system, as horrific as we might believe the system of justice is for adults, I think it is twice as bad for juveniles. I think the lack of intervention early, what drug courts, trying to install a drug court up at Spirit Lake and having jurisdictional issues with a very, very proactive State District Court judge, but still having resistance to doing an interventional court, like a drug court.

So again, it goes back to cultural and historic distrust that drives the inability for us to move forward. And we are going to have to figure out how we can take those steps that build trust that are going to move us forward.

I appreciate your report. I think it really highlights a lot of concerns, not anything I didn't know, having been Attorney General of a State like North Dakota. But the solutions, I find that I have tried a lot of those solutions and have met with resistance and been not able to do it on both sides. And always what gets in the way is trust.

The CHAIRWOMAN. Thank you. Senator Murkowski?

Senator MURKOWSKI. Thank you, Madam Chair.

And thank you to each of you for your testimony and just the level of work that went into it to provide this report from the Commission. That truly is dedication. It is extraordinarily important. The fact that you spent the time on the ground rather than sitting in some nice office, and assuming that you knew what you were hearing from folks being out there on the ground is critically important. So thank you for just your diligence and attention to what I think we all recognize is critically important as we look at these issues, as to how we provide for a level of protection, a level of justice for our First Peoples.

Tamra, your testimony, I will tell you, I sit and I listen to a lot of people with nice titles come, but you spoke from the heart today. You spoke for your children and your grandchildren and all your family, all your Alaska Native families. So thank you for truly giving voice to those who unfortunately too often do not have that voice.

The way you described our conversations with your grandson about not being around on the snow machine when the plane comes in loaded with booze, that is something that as Alaskans we might understand and get it. Folks here in the lower 48 have no concept of what it can mean to be in a small village that is isolated, with no road access, one way in and out, at least for most parts of the area, you might be able to take a boat down the river. But our reality is such that it is beyond the comprehension of most people.

So your testimony today to try to describe how on a daily basis you deal with the realities of a family and a community that lacks basic protection, and you are not asking for a lot of fancy things. But when your closest State trooper is Bethel, isn't that correct?

Ms. TRUETT JERUE. We have Aniak, too.

Senator MURKOWSKI. Okay, so describe for the Committee here, you have a State trooper that is how many miles away?

Ms. TRUETT JERUE. Air miles, about 240 miles, air miles. It is about an hour and 20 minute flight, weather permitting.

Senator MURKOWSKI. Weather permitting. And oftentimes, weather is not permitting.

Ms. TRUETT JERUE. Right.

Senator MURKOWSKI. Your courthouse, the State courthouse is there in Bethel.

Ms. TRUETT JERUE. Yes.

Senator MURKOWSKI. Which is about 400 miles away, maybe?

Ms. TRUETT JERUE. About, 450 miles.

Senator MURKOWSKI. To get to the closest courthouse.

Ms. TRUETT JERUE. Weather permitting.

Senator MURKOWSKI. Weather permitting. The jurors that then come into that courthouse actually have to be flown from other communities.

Ms. TRUETT JERUE. Right. We do get jury notices every once in a while. In the 30 years I have lived there, I have gotten a couple and I have never been flown to Bethel for a trial, except as a witness.

Senator MURKOWSKI. And would they expect you to fund that ticket yourself? What does it cost to fly to Bethel?

Ms. TRUETT JERUE. The cost to fly to Bethel is $750 round trip.

Senator MURKOWSKI. Round trip. And that just gets you to Bethel?

Ms. TRUETT JERUE. Yes, it does.

Senator MURKOWSKI. Madam Chairman, it is important to ask what I think Tamra would consider pretty basic questions, not really about the report. But this is the reality that Alaska Natives live in our rural and remote communities. So when we are talking about providing for a level of protection, it is a different situation. And I listened as the comments were made about being able to at least drive. And it is long distances, I appreciate that. But at least you have the ability to get into a vehicle and move.

Mr. Eid, I want to ask you a couple of questions here in the remaining time that I have. There are some things coming out of this report that I absolutely strongly support. You have the parity in tribal court funding, which I think is imperative. Unfortunately, we sure didn't hear that enthusiasm for that coming from the BIA. But the empowerment of local communities, what we are doing there, and Madam Chairman, I would ask that my opening statement be submitted as part of the record. Because I pointed to some of the opportunities where our local communities are addressing their own issues.

But I guess the biggest question that I have for you, Mr. Eid, is this. We see constantly the description of the failures coming from the reservations in the lower 48. The Washington Post had a big Sunday article talking about some of the failures here.

And in recognizing that, I have to look at the report and say, why are the recommendations for Alaska really moving toward the recreation of Indian reservations, if they are not performing as we want them to be? I am not suggesting that the Alaska situation is acceptable. It is absolutely not. But do we want to take what many would acknowledge is a failed or failing system and then just say, that is the Alaska answer? Try to help me through why you believe that that is the approach? Or maybe it is a hybrid?

Mr. EID. Madam Chair, Senator Murkowski, I really appreciate being here with you and I admire your leadership very much. Let me just say that we don't have to have an Indian reservation system in Alaska to have self-governance. You could have some form of special jurisdiction. In fact, we talk about this in the report, a special Indian Country jurisdiction.

Just so long as the communities have territorial integrity and they can govern themselves, or they can enforce their own laws and be governed by them. What I don't think works is the colonial model in Alaska. And when I say colonial, I am not trying to play to the crowd. My dad grew up in a colonial system in Egypt and came here with a hundred bucks when he was 17, so I kind of know about colonialism. The system in Alaska is not serving the people there, because the State can never police it from afar.

When we were up there last time in December, the leaders came to us and said, we just had a 12 year old girl raped, it took them four days to come out to our village. That is not acceptable in our Country. And I know it is not acceptable to you. It just seems to me that if we can get past what I think is a misnomer or canard about a reservation system, no one is proposing to replicate anything in Alaska other than to say, these are self-governing nations, they are federally-recognized as such under Federal law, enable them to be able to enforce their own laws and be governed by them.

Don't fight with the people when you are a State government. There is no reason for it.

I have great respect for the State of Alaska and for the people there and for the officials who have to make the hard calls. But they shouldn't be fighting with the tribal nations there. They should say, who is the tribal court, here is what we need to enforce a restraining order, now reinforce it. And if there is a problem with the requirements being met, help train them, help get them up to that standard. But don't try to hold it down. Try to build it up.

And I think that is coming in Alaska. I really think that with your leadership and with your colleague, Senator Begich's leadership, I think this can happen. I am really optimistic about it.

Senator MURKOWSKI. Madam Chair, my time is well over. Mr. Eid, I would love the opportunity to pick your brain about some of the proposals contained within the report. I would ask, Madam Chair, that a copy of the Alaska Rural Justice and Law Enforcement Commission, the report that came out in January 2012, be included as part of the record. I don't know whether that was incorporated as part of the Commission's report. But it is an important enough report that I would like to have it included. *

The CHAIRWOMAN. Without objection.

Senator MURKOWSKI. I look forward to further discussions and thank you for coming all this way, Tamra. I so appreciate it.

The CHAIRWOMAN. Thank you.

Senator Tester?

Senator TESTER. [Presiding.] I want to echo Senator Murkowski and say thank you, all of you, for your testimony. I very much appreciate it today, especially yours. That was very good.

The work of the Commission really focused around making jurisdiction divides clearer and ensuring the sovereignty of tribes. So could you share with us, and this can be either Ms. Ellis or Mr. Eid, could you share with us the benefits of having a single appellate court on par with the existing 13 circuit courts?

Mr. EID. Let me just quickly say, Senator Tester, I appreciate very much the question. What we came up with was an idea for a specialized court. It is like the Federal circuit court here in D.C. that hears intellectual property cases. It would be a court where all the Indian Country cases go, so that there would be a consistent body of law and it would be, we think, faster and more expeditious.

So what would happen, sir, is that let's just say someone raised a constitutional challenge in a tribal court proceeding. So you have a criminal defendant who has raised a Fourth Amendment claim, illegal search and seizure, say. So they go into tribal court and the prosecution would occur there, with a tribal prosecutor. Say the person is convicted. Then that defendant would appeal. The first step would be in tribal court, they would exhaust the remedies. That is, they would already go through whatever the appellate process the tribe has.

But the twist that we recommend is the Federal Speedy Trial Act would apply to that. So there is no delay, which happens sometimes in tribal court. Believe me, I litigate there a lot, I know, it

---

* The information referred to has been retained in the Committee files and can be found at *http://akjusticecommission.org/pdf/reports/ARJLEC—2012—Report.pdf*

can happen. So then it gets into the Federal system and it would be a direct appeal, not up through a U.S. district court, but it would go right to an Article 3 U.S. court of appeals, just for this purpose. And then there would be discretionary review to the U.S. Supreme Court.

So the whole idea is make sure that Federal constitutional right is vindicated for every single U.S. citizen. But have it in one place, make it an expedited process and try to ensure that Federal civil rights are enforced.

Senator TESTER. What would be the downside of it?

Mr. EID. The downside is, I have been told, of course I have been told a lot of things by people who are not in your position, so I will look to you for the leadership. But some people think that the Congress would never create another panel or another court, it just sounds too expensive. We are not talking about something that would be more expensive, I don't think, sir. If you had a three-judge panel that could sit in Indian Country, in fact, it could be on the road, it could kind of be the way we were, you could fund these folks through the same process so you could decide whether they were up to that kind of a job or not. But the bottom line is they could go out and they would hear these cases, they would really get good at this, I think, over time.

So there would be a cost involved, there is an up-front cost, there is a fiscal note. But I think in general it is a way to vindicate the right.

Then if I might say also, secondly, a lot of Native people on reservations don't get their full constitutional rights today.

Senator TESTER. Bingo.

Mr. EID. Thus the Indian Civil Rights Act, and it is a travesty, they are American citizens. They should get all their rights, including when the tribal governments abuse their rights. They have Federal civil rights. They should be able to vindicate that.

So let them go into that process too. There may be some opposition, I know, on that issue from tribes. But we all have to live in the same system, and that is part of the price of admission.

Senator TESTER. I appreciate that. While we are talking about the Division of Indian Justice, a new division within the Department of Justice, that would be able to specifically address concerns in tribal courts, Federal districts, overseeing Indian Country and investigations into tribal country. Is that correct? Is that a correct assessment?

Mr. EID. Yes, sir. It would take all those functions that are in the Bureau of Justice Services, Bureau of Indian Affairs Office of Justice Services and combine them into DOJ, along with the group of FBI and so on to do additional enforcement if they are needed.

Senator TESTER. Were you guys able to do any sort of cost assessments on the proposals? We talked a little bit about it on the court.

Mr. EID. Senator Tester, I am glad you asked that. We specifically met with the White House staff in November. They asked us that same question. They said it would help if you would break it all out, which we have done in our testimony here. That way it could go to OMB. So one of the things that would be great, I think they are going to do that, but if you could just please remind them.

They said they put some of these things through OMB. And if we knew what they cost, I think it might help the Committee.

Senator TESTER. Yes, bingo. Just a little bit about the lack of police officers that you address in your testimony, Ms. Ellis. It is something this Committee has talked about before, especially in the large land-based tribes. Are there technological improvements, and if so, what would they be, to help Indian Country, to help bring them into the 21st century when it comes to law enforcement?

Ms. ELLIS. I am just trying to think of all the things I want to talk about when it comes to lack of law enforcement in Indian Country. Just to go back a little bit to Senator Murkowski's point, the situation in the lower 48 is vastly better than it is in Alaska.

Senator TESTER. That is correct. It is not too cheery down here, either.

Ms. ELLIS. No, it is not. But you know, we have heard just resources for ankle monitoring, whether or not tribal courts can actually do some more on the ground technological monitoring to make sure that somebody is not violating the terms of their parole. It really does boil down to a lot of resources. As a fairly conservative person, I don't feel that it was our role to come to Washington and say, let's just keep throwing money at this problem and putting band-aids on it here and there. Our view, and my view, would be let's fix the big problem, get a structure that is working, and then if we can invest in a structure that is working, I think that is something that this entire Congress can get behind.

But right now, we keep investing in a broken system with a whole bunch of band-aids. I don't mean to be general about it, but I am tired of buying band-aids.

Senator TESTER. I appreciate your testimony.

Senator Begich?

Senator BEGICH. Thank you very much.

I am sorry I have had to come in and out. I have had some meetings in the back here.

Tamra, thank you. I know it has taken you four or five days to get here. The sad news, this place shuts down where there is snow. So they say later tonight there might be snow. I don't know when you were planning to go home, but you might be here a little longer than you anticipated. But first, thank you for being here. Thank you for representing Alaska and also tribes not only in our State but around the Country on the issues of justice.

If I can ask you just a couple of questions, and again thank you for your testimony, which I have had a chance to review, so I appreciate that. Let me ask you, first, as you know, I have a bill, the Safe Families and Villages Act, trying to give more power to villages to really handle their justice system. I am a hard core believer in this. I think it is important. Can you give me your thoughts, one, on how tribal courts, in your mind, are successful and where those are working? But also specifically in our bill, we have the repeal of Section 910 of VAWA, and our comments on that, if you would. Then I have a couple other questions.

Ms. TRUETT JERUE. Briefly, in terms of tribal courts, I have worked with tribal courts in terms of child protection a lot in Alaska. We do have some, oftentimes our tribal councils are acting as our courts, or they will have elders as part of those. And I believe that the tribal courts in our small systems have been very effective in those cases. I also believe that they have been very effective in juvenile justice cases, particularly minor infractions and things like that, where there is no monitoring available, there is no probation, there is no fancy program for people to go to. So I think that in small communities where we have a fairly active tribal court, I believe that it can be very effective. Because at that point, you are looking at people you know very, very well. And in knowing them so well, you also know what is happening next door.

Senator BEGICH. What the capacity is and what else is going on in their life or with their family.

Ms. TRUETT JERUE. And I think that there some tribes in Alaska that really do have already some of the infrastructure in place to do that. So that is a brief answer to that question.

Senator BEGICH. Let me, if I can, and you have probably heard me say this publicly, and if you haven't, this is a statement I make a lot of times, on the issues of dealing with tribal courts. Let me pause for a moment, my brother Tom works in this area a lot, throughout the State as you probably know, and as well when I was on Anchorage Assembly, we started Expanded Youth Court, which was founded on the principle of tribal courts and elder courts, or youth and elder courts, which have been great successes, as you just described.

We went in alone, in a way, because we couldn't get the State to step up as I thought they could. So I want to get a sense from you, in working on these issues, how has the State helped or hindered you in these efforts, knowing there is always this thing they always like to talk about, which is sovereignty issues. But in reality, this is about justice. This is about giving opportunities for young people to get on the right track rather than the wrong track.

Can you give me a sense, and if you feel uncomfortable saying it, I understand. But I have had my criticisms, to be frank with you, of the State's inability to really see this as an opportunity.

Ms. TRUETT JERUE. I work, I am a trained social worker, and I have been working in this field for a long time in rural Alaska, that is where I work. Not just in Anvik. I believe that the State has hindered us in many ways from solutions that we could have dealt with there locally.

Senator BEGICH. Solutions you all thought were workable.

Ms. TRUETT JERUE. From the community, whether it is the community council, to the tribal council, to whatever infrastructure may be in place in that community, they have come up with some excellent ideas. But we were then hindered by State intervention and/or lack of. I think that has happened oftentimes, and again, it is not a criticism of the individual State workers.

Senator BEGICH. Understood.

Ms. TRUETT JERUE. It is a criticism of the system itself. It is not working for us out there. I think that as local people, we know our people, we know our resources, we know our limitations. But we also know that there are some times we could be more effective by just purely getting real creative that wouldn't be listed in some system.

So I think it is really important that we get this opportunity to do that.

Senator BEGICH. We have seen wellness courts, youth courts, tribal courts, a variety of new approaches that have shown success. If you have more flexibility, less lack of access or ability, you can do a lot of things. Is that a fair statement? Or at least try some things that might give some avenue of opportunity to solve some of these problems?

Ms. TRUETT JERUE. We have done just that. We got a CTAS grant that was a youth court grant for Anvik. I helped write that grant. Then when we actually received the funding, it was wonderful and we were very grateful for that. But re-looking at the grant, when it was written, it required that we have a mental health person or somebody come in and be working with our kids. Well, I have only seen a mental health person in Anvik in, well, I don't know, I have lived there 25 years, maybe once. So I figured, well, this isn't going to work for us, even though we could make it work.

So what I did is I talked to several people in the community and I said, you know what would really work more effectively is a peer mentoring group. And that would look different in our community than it is going to look in the community 20 miles upriver, because they have some different issues than we have.

So we rewrote it, and they accepted that. How ours looks is that we work with the kids from the age of 6 until 20. And we make sure they have activities, we make sure that they are being supervised in those activities and we are talking to our teenagers and really teaching them about the fact that they are also tribal citizens. They don't know that.

Senator BEGICH. Let me say this, I am over my time. I did have questions for the Commissioners, but I will submit those. I know we have talked, and I want to first commend you guys. You did an incredible report. Not that we look to be seeing the kind of information that comes out of it, but what it is, it is an eye opener for us and what we need to do, what we need to be acting on. This is not a report that that should end up on some shelf somewhere collecting more dust until we sit here five years later having the same conversation.

I want to commend you guys for doing it, one, that there was unanimous support of the report. It wasn't politicized, it was, here is what you saw. Here is what is happening and here is what we think. Some solutions were not in detail in the sense that we need to this, because I know you want to get down that path.

But I want to say thank you for doing this. For Alaska, it is tough love sometimes when we have to see these things. But it is good for us to be reminded of how far we still have to go when it comes to justice systems in Alaska. So thank you for that.

I will submit some questions for the record, because I know my colleagues are—it is 5:30. I know Tamra would stay here as long as she wants, because she is five days flying here and only five minutes. I don't know if that ratio worked out fairly for her. But we just really appreciate Tamra for being here. Thank you for being here, Tamra, again, for five days on a plane. I try to explain this to my colleagues all the time. Thank you for being the example of what we talk about all the time.

The CHAIRWOMAN. [Presiding.] Do my colleagues have more questions?

Senator Murkowski?

Senator MURKOWSKI. Madam Chairman, I don't have a question, but I want to share an article, a CNN report from February 6th. * It highlights a 104-year old Alaska Native woman, Elsie Nanugaq Tommy, who is 104 years old, who has started a women's shelter. They call it a secret women's shelter, in Newtok. And Denise Tommy, who is over there, the women's coalition in Bethel, talking about the shelters. But the point of sharing this with you is, the report says Alaska doesn't have to be the State where rape is most common, that we can do small things to make a difference. And we have talked about community empowerment.

But I am looking at some of these suggestions: donate to worthy organizations like shelters, start a petition to get cops in every village, tell your story, host a choose respect rally, demand rape kits are counted, share this post with your friends. We have incredible, incredible issues that face us in rural Alaska. Our statistics are staggering and sobering. To think that these are some of the solutions that we are looking at, share this post with your friends, start a petition, donate to worthy organizations, I think we need to, as policy makers, do that much more to redouble our efforts to make a difference. Because as genuine and heartfelt as starting a petition is, we have some real problems we have to deal with.

Thank you for letting me share that.

The CHAIRWOMAN. Senator Tester?

Senator TESTER. Tank you, Madam Chair.

On a completely different issue, I would say you were very complimentary to us earlier in this meeting. The last Committee meeting we had, we bid you adieu.

This is your last Committee meeting, and I just want to say thank you for your service, not only to Indian Country, but to the Country and you will remain on this Committee, and hopefully be an active member of it. We thank you very much for your service.

The CHAIRWOMAN. Thank you. My heart is definitely with this Committee, and I want to thank the staff on both sides for their hard work. I have really enjoyed working with all of you.

Boy, I get a gavel after what, less than a year?

[Laughter.]

The CHAIRWOMAN. I want to say, I have every confidence that Senator Tester, who represents tens of thousands of Native Americans, will do an outstanding job on this Committee, because he is so steeped in these policy issues, traveling around his State. I just know that all of these issues he has dealt with. He will bring great leadership to this Committee. That is what makes it, I am not saying easy to move over, but the Small Business Committee does have some interest in Native American issues. So we will look forward to working with this Committee on those.

I want to thank you again for this hearing. It is a very important hearing, a very important public policy issue. You came with some good suggestions, we will try to get them implemented. Thank you.

---

* The information referred to has been retained in the Committee files and can be found at http://www.cnn.com/2014/02/03/opinion/sutter-alaska-rape-change/.

We are adjourned.
[Applause.]
[Whereupon, at 5:40 p.m., the Committee was adjourned.]

APPENDIX

PREPARED STATEMENT OF IVAN D. POSEY, CHAIRMAN, MONTANA-WYOMING TRIBAL
LEADERS COUNCIL

Good afternoon. My name is Ivan D. Posey and I currently serve on the Eastern Shoshone Business Council from the Wind River Indian Reservation located in Wyoming. I also serve as Chairman for the Montana-Wyoming Tribal Leaders Council which consists of seven tribes in Montana, two tribes in Wyoming and the Shoshone-Bannock tribe in Idaho.

It is an honor to provide testimony to the Senate Committee on Indian Affairs regarding the Indian Law and Order Commission report regarding a ''Roadmap for Making Native America Safer'' which was released in November 2013. Many times I have had the opportunity to provide testimony to this distinguished committee which includes my own Senator, John Barrasso.

My testimony today will focus on Juvenile Justice: Failing the Next Generation.

The report outlines many serious issues with the juvenile justice system in Indian Country and the lack of resources needed to address these concerns. From jurisdictional, detention, treatment and educational barriers, to name a few, the obstacles pertaining to tribal youth are still outstanding.

First, let me address detention. Many tribes lack adequate facilities to house juvenile offenders that may pose a risk to public safety, and in many instances, their own safety. Some juveniles, who may be intoxicated, are sometimes returned to the home where safety becomes a concern for family members who dwell there. On the Wind River Indian Reservation, some adjudicated youth are sent to a detention facility two hours away in Sweetwater County or detained for a longer period in Busby, Montana, which is four hours away. There are no local facilities to hold juveniles.

Many of these youth may not be criminally inclined but may suffer from health related issues such as Post Traumatic Stress Disorder. The need for stronger mental health services in Indian Country is paramount. When these services are available, through referral, voluntary or through the school systems, they would drastically prevent many tribal youth from entering the juvenile justice system and incarceration. Services need to be enhanced, or made available, and designed to work with the entire family which is affected.

As noted in the report, jurisdictional matters regarding tribal youth may be better served for hearing in tribal courts. Of course that depends on the capacity of some courts and the ability to monitor and evaluate outcomes. There are some ways to effectively address and prevent further detention through family and drug courts for youth offenders. The ability to create models through traditional and cultural values is a very real possibility in the tribal court systems. Over the years I have seen tribal youth lost in the system and when they become adults they are prosecuted in the federal system and serve time in a federal institution.

Second, let me address services to families, and in some instances, extended families. There have been many programs available in Indian Country to address these concerns over the years; many have been effective while some have gone to the wayside. Boys and Girls Clubs, United National Indian Tribal Youth (UNITY) and other programs have stood the test of time and continue to be effective in Indian Country. These programs create a sense of belonging and contribution which is very important to young people. As in any successful endeavor, family participation is very important. From parent/teacher conferences to volunteering for youth activities, participation from parents or guardians remains low. To be effective there has to be a holistic approach to family involvement in the lives of our youth.

Although at times, there is a sense of shame and guilt associated when dealing with youth issues, there has to be a more effective approach to working with families in their homes. It is likened to a person who attends treatment but returns to the same environment. Part of the problem may lie with a caring parent who feels they have no control or resources to address the issue regarding their child or grandchild. This would give the adults the opportunity to seek help and have a strong support system to assist them.

Suicide Prevention has also been effective in many tribal communities. Decades ago the subject was not openly discussed in our tribal communities even though it was a common occurrence. We have lost too many of our tribal youth to suicide and many families still live with the pain and emptiness of how they may have prevented it. Myself, I have lost two nephews and one niece to suicide.all of them my older brother's children.

Third, the educational system needs to teach our children instead of testing. Testing sometimes make our children feel alienated if they are not in a certain category or group. Individualism needs to be recognized and commended. Many schools are faced with children who have Fetal Alcohol Effects (FAE) and require special needs such as Individual Educational Plans (IEP) which require more one on one teaching. Many of these children receive great educational services but some may not. Schools have a huge responsibility regarding the development of our children and preventing many from becoming part of the juvenile justice system.

Although the problems may seem insurmountable at times, I am optimistic that positive change can happen in Indian Country regarding Juvenile Justice. This report has outlined the barriers and has created a pathway to address and overcome the many obstacles tribal youth face. Many answers lie within our communities and our tribal people. We need to continue to strengthen what works and embrace positive change.

As in any society our youth need a sense of belonging and feel that their contribution is being acknowledged. We all have our own "medicine" and we contribute in a positive or negative manner. A young child is not destined to be a juvenile offender and detained in a system where they may become introduced to a harsher way of life. Many of our children have been through a life of violence, substance abuse, sexual assaults and suicides . . . as tribal communities it is time to act and make our youth feel that they have a voice, are being heard, and their contributions are being recognized. Through prevention, family involvement, community support and innovative means of discipline, our tribal youth have a bright future.

WHO WEE HOO and GOD bless.

PREPARED STATEMENT OF THE GREAT PLAINS TRIBAL CHAIRMAN'S ASSOCIATION

Madame Chairwoman and Members of the Committee:

Thank you for holding this important hearing and for allowing the Great Plains Tribal Chairman's Association (GPTCA) to present the following preliminary observations and comments on the Tribal Law and Order Commission's (TLOC) final report. We would also like to thank the Members of the Commission for their hard work and dedication.

More Hearings and BIA Meetings Are Necessary

Nothing is more important to the Members of the GPTCA than the safety and security of our members. For that reason, we encourage this Committee to hold additional hearings on the Commission's report in order to receive testimony from as many tribal leaders as possible. Additionally, because the resolution of many of the problems discussed in this report will require the concurrence and active participation of the Senate Judiciary Committee, we would hope that some of those hearings could be conducted jointly by your two Committees.

We would also ask this Committee to encourage the BIA to begin holding comprehensive meetings with Tribal leaders, tribal judges and tribal law enforcement officers to discuss these important findings and recommendations. It is our hope that senior representatives from OMB, the Department of Justice (DOJ) and the Indian Health Service (IHS) will participate in these events because their cooperation is clearly going to be required to implement many of the Commission's recommendations.

We Also Need the Participation of the Budget and Apppropriations Committees

We further ask you to help us assure the participation of the Members of the House and Senate Budget and Appropriations Committees in your hearings. Many positive public safety changes have been authorized in recent years, but the appropriations required to implement those changes have not been forthcoming. We need to find a way to change that, because the absence of these much needed appropriations has left major differences between what was authorized by this Committee, and what has and can be implemented by most of the Tribal Nations in the Great Plains.

This is evidenced by what has happened with the expanded tribal sentencing and tribal jurisdiction provisions of the Tribal Law and Order Act (TLOA) and the Violence Against Women Act (VAWA). While some economically-successful gaming tribes have recently announced that they have already amended their tribal Codes and hired professional judges, prosecutors and defense attorneys, using their own third party income and are now preparing to implement the expanded tribal jurisdiction authorized by TLOA and VAWA, such is not the case for the majority of tribes in the Great Plains. In fact, for most Great Plains Tribes as well as most other treaty tribes, who are among the poorest in the United States, the idea of funding the pre-requisites required to expand their sentencing authority and tribal criminal jurisdiction is outside the realm of possibility. As a result, many of the members of those tribes now view these much talked about authorizations in TLOA and VAWA as nothing but another set of unfulfilled promises. This is wrong, especially when you consider that the Treaty and Large Land Based Reservations we are talking about house the largest percentage of on-reservation Indians in the United States.

Now let us turn to some specific comments on the TLOA Commission's Recommendations.

Tribal Jurisidiction Over Non-Indians Needs to be Returned Now!

We were thrilled to see that the Commission's first recommendation was to allow those tribes, who chose to do so, a path toward again exercising criminal jurisdiction over non-Indians who commit crimes in their tribal homelands. The Commission was absolutely right when it concluded that on-reservation criminal justice should be controlled locally by the Tribe, and that the Supreme Court's decision to take away tribal jurisdiction over non-Indian perpetrators has created nothing but problems. This Committee has heard hours of testimony on this point during its hearings on TLOA.

Too many of our tribal people are injured by the actions of non-Indians who we lack the practical ability to control. We find it disheartening that so much Congressional attention remains focused on protecting the civil rights of the non-Indian perpetrator while so little attention is focused on defending the civil rights of the Indian victim. Returning criminal jurisdiction over non-Indians to those Tribes who wish to exercise it is the most cost effective and practical way of correcting these problems. In 2014, no tribe should have less practical ability to protect its citizens than the average small town in the United States.

At the same time, we are disheartened by the fact that the Commission's recommendations again tie our ability to exercise this inherent sovereign authority to our ability to pay for tribal court pre-requisites which we cannot afford, and which the Federal Government has never chosen to fund. Four years after the passage of TLOA, our courts have not only failed to receive any real increases in federal dollars; they have actually lost ground because of sequestration. So, if you continue to follow this same path, you will again find yourself making an offer which only those tribes with sizable third party incomes will be able to accept.

Because some tribes are preparing to begin exercising expanded jurisdiction under VAWA, we felt it was necessary to stress the importance of assuring that those tribes are provided the federal support and resources they will need to defend that jurisdiction. We know that as soon as the first non-Indian is brought before a tribal criminal court legal challenges will quickly follow. These challenges will most likely lead to long and very expensive litigation which will not only bring the scope of tribal criminal jurisdiction and inherent tribal sovereignty squarely before the federal courts, but will also establish a precedent for what can and will happen within other tribal Nations across the United States.

Improvements in the Federal Judiciary

We were also pleased to see that the Commission has recommended that the federal courts begin holding federal criminal trials, involving Indian defendants, on or near our reservations. Most of our federal courts are located hours from our tribal communities. We have no public transportation to those locations and our people lack the practical ability to travel to those sites. Thus, federal criminal trials involving on-reservation crime are often viewed by our members as actions that are being taken by and for outsiders.

We were equally happy to see the Commission's call for the renewed use of Indian Federal Magistrates. We do not need another expensive study to determine the worth of this program, that worth has already been proven. We just need you to make the program permanent and available to those tribes that wish to utilize it. We have a number of tribal members who have all of the legal education and experience necessary to serve in these positions. We would hope that you would direct the

Federal Government to look to these individuals as potential candidates to fill those positions. We would also note that if this program is going to be as effective and well received as possible, each Tribe should have a direct role in the selection and approval of the Magistrate who will serve their community.

We also feel strongly that a tribe should continue to play a direct role in the selection of the special Assistant U.S. Attorney who will serve as its liaison. As we discuss below, we currently have an excellent working relationship with the individuals who serve in these positions in the Great Plains, but we also know that these individuals will change over time. We must continue to play a direct role in the selection of their replacements to further advance our relationship with the U.S. Attorney's Office.

Finally, we support the Commission's call for an expanded tribal role in federal and state prosecutorial decisions. The participation of Tribal Prosecutors in federal criminal trials, authorized by TLOA, has already proven its worth, and that participation should continue to be expanded. Too many of our people are in federal prison for crimes that would have been better handled in our tribal court systems or by being sentenced to treatment rather than just incarceration.

When a Tribal member is convicted in federal court, or when a federal plea agreement is contemplated, the Tribal prosecutor should also be given a direct role in deciding the proposed sentence even if they did not participate in the case. Most of these convicted individuals are going to return to our tribal communities, and we should therefore have a tribal voice in deciding the disposition of these matters.

Juvenile Justice

We were very happy that the Commission devoted considerable time and attention to the issue of juveniles. Too many of our children find themselves caught up in the federal and tribal criminal justice systems. More often than not, their actions were influenced, at least in part, by something going on or not going on at home. We agree that juvenile incarceration should be seen as a last resort, but we must advise this Committee that we do have some juveniles who require highly supervised residential attention and we cannot eliminate completely the use of juvenile detention centers.

One of the big problems we currently face is our lack of residential programs for children who are simply in need of care and supervision, and for juveniles who are repeat status offenders. We recognize that if care and attention is not provided, or if that care and attention is not sensitive to their tribal culture, too many of these young people will find themselves in the criminal justice system at some point in their life. In fact, most Indian people who are currently incarcerated started out as neglected youth or status offenders who lost track of their tribal heritage and belief systems. We might have been able to prevent this from happening if we would have just had the resources available to intervene when they were still children. While we recognize that group homes and culturally centered counseling and residential treatment locations are not normally viewed as a part of the "criminal" justice system, they should be viewed as major crime prevention tools which are well worth the cost.

We also agree that the Tribe should be notified and allowed to become a full partner in all judicial decisions whenever a tribal juvenile is brought into any State or Federal criminal justice system. State and Federal Courts often do not understand the circumstances that led a juvenile to act the way they did, and they also fail to recognize some of the tribal tools available to address the situation. For example, many State and Federal Courts do not understand or appreciate the role that a child's extended family members play in tribal society, or how extended family members can be used to help redirect the life of a child. So please help us stop future crime by helping us redirect the lives of juveniles who, without tribal and federal assistance, may end up before the adult criminal courts.

Cross-Deputization Agreements

No Tribe should feel pressured or be coerced into entering into an inter-governmental policing agreement with a non-Indian government simply because they have inadequate funds to operate their own law enforcement and corrections programs. Additionally, no tribe should be penalized or looked down upon for refusing to do so. Each tribe has a different present and historical relationship with its surrounding governments and as such each tribe should remain totally free to decide for itself how to handle matters of this importance.

At the same time, we support the Commission's call for removing some of the current impediments to such agreements—like insurance—for those tribes who are interested in exploring these options.

Flexible Funding—Not Block Grants

Because our tribes have diverse needs, we support the Commissions' call for a "flexible" funding system which allows tribes to decide for themselves where to put the federal public safety and justice money that they receive. We need a single source of adequate base funding, and what we are receiving from BIA today does not even come close to meeting anyone's definition of adequate.

At the same time, we are extremely concerned about the Commission's call for the use of block grants as the mechanism for achieving this goal. Block grants are designed to assist and supplement the funding needs of a government which already has a viable tax base and the ability to run a basic program. Block grants were designed to provide a federal means to enhance those programs, not to be their sources of basic operating dollars. Thus, they are not the answer for tribal programs that do not have, and have never had, a reasonable source of base funding.

Federal block grant allocations are always based on formulas which, by their very nature, can never really consider the actual needs of a given community. Block grants also provide no mechanism for addressing changed circumstances, or emergency funding needs, and no viable mechanism for assisting a tribe to catch its programs up to the level that others have already achieved. We are already experiencing these exact same problems with our current block grant programs for roads and housing construction. Law Enforcement, courts and public safety cannot work in this manner.

The BIA's current base funding for law enforcement and courts is totally flawed because it has always been distributed disproportionate to actual need. To make matters worse, the percentages given to the tribes in the Great Plains and other large land based and treaty tribes are far below those received by many other tribes in the U.S. There is no fair and honest "distribution formula." Tribes which were recognized in more recent years, and tribes who received tribal court and public safety add-ons in the 1970s thru the early 1990s, have been able to increase their base funding to a still inadequate, but a least more reasonable level, while ours has remained stagnant.

Additionally, many of our tribes suffer a disproportionate impact on their base budgets when the costs of gasoline and other similar items go up. Our large land based tribes not only have higher gasoline costs, because of the miles that their emergency vehicles have to be driven each day. They also have higher annual vehicle maintenance cost because of excess mileage and bad roads, and their police vehicles have a shorter life span. Thus, even when law enforcement funding has remained stable, our large land based tribes have still seen their base budgets fall further behind every single year. A block grant program that does not have the ability to adjust to these very real annual changes is going to leave us in an even worse position than we already are today.

It is also important for us to note, that unlike some other tribes in the Country, the funding for our Great Plains public safety programs stems directly from the treaty commitments that U.S. government made. The very language in our treaties calls for the actual protection of our communities, not just for a share of an insufficient block grant program that fails to achieve that objective.

Parity has to Have a Realistic Meaning

We are also pleased that the Commission has emphasized the need for parity in our law enforcement staffing, but we define "parity" in a far different way. To us "parity" means the minimum staffing currently existing in a community of comparable population, comparable land base, comparable economic conditions, and comparable social problems, which has had the resources available to it to make an informed decision on the level of protection that needs to be provided to address those conditions. Not on some abstract comparison of population to officers. Today, our police departments remain funded at 50 percent of what the Federal Government itself has determined to be our actual need. This is one of the reasons that we started our testimony by calling for a "buy-in" to the Commission's recommendations by OMB and the House and Senate Budget and Appropriations Committees. Simply saying we need more officers is not getting the job done.

Additionally, comparing many of our reservations to the average small American town does not work. Unlike most rural communities, many of our reservations in the Great Plains are the size of some states. They have far more widely dispersed residential communities, far more serious alcohol and drug problems, far higher drop out and suicide rates, far higher unemployment and poverty levels, and jurisdictional issues that are far more complicated than those which exist in most rural communities in the United States.

Indian country also has a number of unique situations which call for a special definition of parity. The best example of this is the MHA Tribal Nation which because of the oil and gas boom, now has more transient workers living in some of its communities than tribal members. It also has 20,000 large oil and gas trucks per day traveling at high rates of speed on the same dilapidated roads used by school children and local residents. This has created a huge public safety crisis in that community which the current BIA funding system has no ability to address. In fact, traffic is not even a factor that is taken into consideration when BIA funding is distributed. Because these situations have been ignored by BIA, crime has risen significantly at MHA, at the same time that federal dollars have been cut back. This is not the way a federal public safety program should be operated. Simply put, these are the types of very real factors that the BIA's current 3.8 officers to 1,000 people formulas fails to consider and that cannot, and most likely will not, be factored into a federal block grant formula. Parity means parity with other identical communities, not with the average rural town in the United States. An officer in a small rural community in South Dakota, which is 20 miles by 20 miles, can respond to four police calls in the time that it takes an officer at Rosebud to respond to one call which is 60 miles away. An officer in the average rural community may see one or two suicides in a year, while our officers see two or more a month. An officer in most rural areas may get 100 police calls a month; our officers get 100 calls on a single Saturday night, and the average small town does not have traffic and transient issue the come anywhere close to what is happening on the Reservation of the MHA Tribal Nation. These simple realities need to be factored into any "parity" allocation that is developed.

Additionally, parity cannot be measured on just the number of officers required. There are a number of additional costs which have to be considered. Each officer that is added will require a vehicle capable of handling our bad roads, a uniform, training, a number of pieces of equipment and a variety of other things that are both necessary and very expensive. "Parity" can only be achieved when all of these factors are considered.

Finally, we are troubled that the Commission failed to call for "parity" in the staffing, equipping, and funding of our tribal courts and detention programs. We are never going to be able to adequately address crime in our Tribal Nations until these two programs are viewed as being equally essential to that effort. Today, our Courts are operating under conditions that would be viewed as totally unacceptable in any county in the United States. At MHA, the tribe's one tribal judge and one tribal prosecutor have in excess of 3,800 open cases, most of which are drug related and many of which involve drug sales, not just drug possession. No non-Indian prosecutor in this country has 3,800 open criminal cases of this magnitude, and no judge can assure justice to the parties involved in that many different matters.

While non-Indian courts are developing a variety of new and creative ways of administering justice, our tribal courts are struggling just to stay open. Today, our tribal courts lack the basic equipment, training dollars, and court personnel found in every county court in the United States. They also operate without access to the same types of viable treatment, counseling, and other diversion programs common to all other State and county courts in the United States. The end result is, that today, a tribal judge in the Great Plains is forced to decide between incarcerating or releasing a defendant, even when that Judge knows that neither of those alternatives are in the best interest of the tribe or beneficial to crime prevention. We have far too many repeat offenders and we need culturally oriented counseling and treatment programs run by the Tribe if we are really going to make a dent in those statistics.

Stop the Reliance on DOJ Grants and Move the Money Back to BIA Today

We were also pleased to see that the Commission has joined us in opposing the continued use of DOJ grant funding to pay for core law enforcement and court operations. Their findings mirror the statements we have been making for the last twenty-five years.

No one can run a police department or a court on grants, especially when those grants do not become available to even apply for until the last quarter of the fiscal year. We are mandated to start our law enforcement programs on October 1, regardless! We cannot wait until a grant cycle is initiated. Grants are unreliable, we never know if or when we are going to get them, or how much they will be, and our funding needs change radically when we have an emergency like a blizzard, a tornado or even an unexpected influx of drugs. Grants are not flexible enough to address any of these kinds of needs. So please, if you want to advance tribal law enforcement and court operations today, without adding a penny to the taxpayers burden, get together with the members of the Judiciary Committee and the Commerce Justice Appropriations Subcommittee and move the Indian funding from the DOJ's Bureau of Justice Assistance and COPS programs, including all of the construction dollars, back to BIA where they can be used more effectively to meet the actual needs of tribal programs on those reservations which have exclusive tribal/federal jurisdiction.

By doing this you will also be able to undo a DOJ detention and tribal court construction program which has created nothing but problems for the majority of tribes which exercise full criminal jurisdiction on their tribal lands.

We make this recommendation because we know that federal money is tight and hard decisions have to be made. In a perfect world, we would love to see both full funding at BIA for our on-going public safety programs and a reasonable level of DOJ grants which could be used to fund new and unique initiatives. Unfortunately, we do not currently live in a perfect fiscal world.

Our Strong Opposition to Moving Law Enforcement, Courts and Detention to DOJ

While we support the idea of funding all tribal law enforcement, detention and court programs through a single agency, we strongly disagree with the Commission's recommendation for moving BIA law enforcement, courts and detention funding, including construction funding authority, to the DOJ. We will continue to take this same position even if the DOJ grant programs are replaced with permanent on-going funding, and even if DOJ provides the option of "638" contracts. This same BIA to DOJ transfer recommendation has been made three times in the last twenty years and the Tribes have rejected it every time!

DOJ has never exhibited a comprehensive knowledge or practical understanding of on-reservation needs, thus, it lacks the information and understanding necessary to perform this function. How can an agency which is not involved with such important matters as on-reservation land ownership, changes in tribal law, changes in tribal enrollment policies, tribal religious and cultural events and beliefs, the internal problems at tribal schools, and the inter-relationship between programs and services ever going to be capable of managing on-reservation public safety.

DOJ is an agency which has experience dealing in one area- felonies- not with the types of day to day crimes which plague most of our communities. Even their efforts to collect crime statistics on our reservations have failed miserably, because they focus their efforts on felonies and violent crime, while totally ignoring the drunken drivers, incidents of domestic disputes, thefts, traffic problems, fights, and drunk and disorderly cases which are every day occurrences in our Tribal Nations. In fact, they are not even interested in drug arrests in our communities unless the quantity of the drugs seized is above a certain amount.

Simply put, the DOJ's policy makers and law enforcement staff do not have the time and therefore, do want to be bothered with DUI's, shoplifting, stolen household items and fights at basketball games and bars. In fact, they consider most thefts in our tribal communities to be minor offenses, because the value of what is stolen does not rise to the level of a "major theft". I can assure you; however, that the person who lost the only car they have in their entire family, the theft of that car is a major theft—even though that car may only have a blue book value of $500 or less. While we need expanded FBI and other DOJ assistance to address the felonies which do occur on our reservations, this is not the only type of law enforcement and the only type of law enforcement thinking that we need overseeing our police functions.

We are constantly faced with proposals, from well-intended agencies and individuals, which call for the removal of a program or service from the BIA, even though it is the BIA which has the primary responsibility to implementing the federal trust responsibility. We call this "stovepiping" and we oppose all of these proposals outright because they simply do not work.

What the proponents of these ideas fail to understand is that when you live in isolated, impoverished communities like ours, everything is inter-related and what happens in one area impacts another. An after school program get closed down and we see a rise in crimes involving young people. An after school program gets added and we have more accidents because we have more young people walking on our roads after dark. General assistance checks are cut back and we see an increase in drop-out rates and suicide. Agencies like DOJ do not understand this because they lack a comprehensive point of reference. DOJ, by its nature, like to compartmentalize things like this and focus attention on just one area—law enforcement and criminal justice. The BIA and tribal governments, on the other hand, have responsibility for the whole picture.

Managing that whole picture will become more difficult if you remove a vital program like law enforcement from the overall decisions of tribal government, and from the tribal BIA budget process. Crime will not be properly address if DOJ is forced to make decisions on law enforcement while playing no role in the other programs and decisions that impact its success.

At DOJ we are always going to be seen as a lower priority, simply because of that agency's other very important obligations. Some of our tribes recently an issue with another division at DOJ, and it took them seven weeks to get a meeting with the Director. This was not because he was slighting us in any way, or because we doubt for a minute his commitment to tribal leaders or the commitment of Attorney General Holder. That Director just had too many other pressing national concerns to address before he could get to what was on the national scale a small tribal issue impacting only a small number of people. We understand that, and see it as another reason to keep our criminal justice programs at BIA.

Our point about different agency priorities is evidenced in HHS' implementation of its role under TLOA. While Tribes and the BIA recognize the direct relationship between our lack of on-reservation residential alcohol and substance abuse treatment centers and on-reservation crime, HHS has not given that issue the same level of attention. This is evidenced by the fact that, despite all of the studies and all of the testimony the Congress has received over the last twenty-five years, HHS has still not created, or even proposed the creation of, a single residential treatment center in Indian county. We do not want a non-Indian thinking police department and court program coming out of DOJ, it's just that simple.

Finally, it is important for us to note that while we currently enjoy a fine working relationship with our current U.S. Attorneys, and with the DOJ Executives and staff in the Central Office, this has not always been the case. We also know that many of those people will be gone after the next election, regardless of who gets elected. History has taught us that unlike with the BIA, which is well recognized as having a unique trust responsibility, and which has as its sole responsibility the protection of tribal rights; the decision makers in the DOJ are always going to have other responsibilities and other competing priorities. For these reasons alone, the degree of attention they focus on tribal issues will always change over time. This is not a politically motivated statement, it has happened more than once under both Republican and Democratic Administrations. This is why we feel so strongly that we need to maintain and enhance the role of the BIA, rather than creating a new, less effective agency in the DOJ.

Detention

While we were pleased that the Commission touched on the need for additional detention facilities in Indian Country, we are not in agreement with all of its recommendations. In fact, many of those recommendations—and the current discussions which are already underway—scare us a great deal.

When agency officials, academics and Members of Congress discuss "detention" they often think in terms of prisons and long term holding facilities. And, when they talk in terms of "alternatives to incarceration" they are often thinking about persons who are sentenced to long-term incarceration. We have those needs, and we are open to new ideas in those areas, but what we also have is a real need for what most people would think of as the county and municipal jails. Simply put, we need a safe place to put the individual who is drunk and aggressive, the individual who is driving under the influence, the individual who is threatening to beat up another person, and the individual who has just robbed a local store or taken another member's car. We also need a safe local place to keep the individual who is pre-arraignment, the person in or awaiting trial and the person awaiting bail. For many Great Plains Tribes this is not a small number of people.

Additionally, because of our rural isolation, bad roads, and lack of public transportation, we are strongly opposed to the idea of placing even our sentenced offenders hundreds of miles from their families, friends, religious advisors and support groups. The Commission noted the importance of allowing tribes to develop re-entry programs designed to help bring these people back into our communities, and this whole concept is lost if we break family and community ties by incarcerating our people hundreds of miles from home. This is especially true for juveniles.

Unfortunately, Washington being what it is, the very second that the BIA and DOJ started talking about "alternatives to incarceration" and "regional facilities," all discussions surrounding our current local large land base and isolated community needs fell to the wayside and so did the funding to meet those needs. Today, we talk to appropriators about the need to replace our jails, and they tell us that the new emphasis is on "alternatives to incarceration" and "regional facilities." What these individuals fail to recognize is that the majority of the people our law enforcement officers deal with have an underlying alcohol or substance abuse problem, so things like ankle bracelets are not the answer. Treatment is a wonderful long term approach that we strongly support, but it is not a quick solution to our immediate problem. Until that treatment can change the lives of every person within the boundaries of our tribal Nations, we are still going to need local jails to protect our communities. We really wonder if the BIA and DOJ people who are talking about replacing jail space with ankle bracelets understand that there are a sizable percentage of Indian perpetrators who live 60 miles from the closest police substation in areas that the large land based tribes can only patrol sporadically. We also wonder if they understand that many of these areas still do not have phones or Internet, and satellite coverage only work there if the weather is perfectly clear. SO, while we welcome these alternatives to incarceration for tribes which will find them helpful, this is not a comprehensive solution to our problems.

Today, many of the jail and court house facilities in the Great Plains are so deteriorated that they cannot be repaired, and those closest ''jail'' or ''court house'' space that most of our tribes could possibly rent is over 100 miles away. When we say deteriorated, we are talking about heating systems that fail regularly in our 10 degree or below winters, cooling systems that fail regularly in our 90 degree plus summers, and water systems that shut down altogether multiple times per year. Both our tribal and federal employees are working in jail and court house buildings that would be closed down immediately if OSHA officials ever visited them. So, if something is not done about these problems we will have no choice but to start releasing dangerous people back into our communities.

We have so many problems with the current DOJ construction grant programs we could fill pages. So all we can do is highlight some of the most glaring. First, there is no priority list, so tribes which have the most pressing needs find themselves competing against tribes which are just now starting their police forces. Second, DOJ does not provide the core funding for our detention and court staff and does not understand what can and cannot be done with the existing BIA funds, so it is funding the construction of buildings that cannot be staffed. Third, because of the size of some of our populations, the cost of constructing a single justice center in the Great Plains and on other large land based reservations exceeds the entire amount in the DOJ construction budget, and DOJ currently has no mechanism to multi-year fund one of these projects.

The most pressing example of this is the need for a new jail facility at Kyle on the Pine Ridge Reservation. As some of you are aware, the Kyle facility has been at the top of the BIA's jail construction priority list for many years. To address this crisis, the Congress reprogrammed FY 2011 funding to plan and design a new Kyle Justice Center, and directed that this facility be designed to serve the entire eastern side of the Pine Ridge Reservation. Unfortunately, when the facility planners, who included both tribal and BIA law enforcement and court officials, examined the actual occupancy rates at the current Kyle facility, along with the actual number of residents of the eastern side of the Reservation who were currently before the courts, and used those number to project the future needs of such a facility over the next ten years, they quickly determined that a much larger facility was needed in order to meet actual and projected needs of that community for just short term holding. This facility is estimated to cost in excess of $45 million, which is $15 million higher than the maximum amount which has ever been in the DOJ tribal facilities construction budget. The result is that today there is no existing federal program which has the money and the capability of building, or even completing the design on, the highest priority project in Indian Country. DOJ cannot multi-year fund a large project like this, as the BIA was able to do in the past, and no decent contractor is going to want to enter into a contract to build half a building. Even if they were, they certainly are not going to warrant their work. This is a real problem, because Pine Ridge is not the only high priority project which is going to face this problem. Lastly, it is almost impossible to project the actual costs associated with constructing a building as complicated as this with 100 percent accuracy especially given the ever changing federal detention standards. Under the old BIA ''pipeline'' funding, BIA always had funding for future projects which could be dipped into to fund cost overruns and unforeseen problems that developed on on-going construction sites when everyone agreed that those costs needed to be paid. The money was just moved from one project to another. Today, when a DOJ grant faces a similar cost altering problem, the Tribe has to shut the project down or leave it incomplete until the next funding cycle comes up, and it can compete for a new grant, which might or might not be forthcoming, to complete the work. This is a ridiculous and very expensive way to address a federal problem of this magnitude.

Finally, DOJ lacks the practical ability to provide comprehensive advice and technical assistance on these projects for the same reasons we have discussed above. They do not understand our communities, so they cannot predict changes that are likely to occur in things like tribal enrollment and new tribal housing development locations, and the expansion of gangs. They also don't understand tribal land and utility issues, and this becomes a major problem when we run into a need for additional land for a lagoon, a drainage system or a different access point, or when our project is going to have a direct impact on the existing tribal water system or tribal lagoon. They understand how to calculate the relationship between occupancy and space requirements but they do not understand how to calculate projected occupancy rates because they lack a practical understanding of potential changes in tribal law. We could go on, but as you can see, this is not the right place to house these dollars if the Congress wants to obtain the maximum benefits for the least amount of money. So please, help us get the BIA back into the jail and court house construction business now, because what you are currently doing is not working and makes no sense whatsoever.

Alaska

What is going on in Alaska is appalling and needs to be addressed immediately. While Alaskan tribes and Native villages have a different legal relationship with the United States, this fact should not be used as an excuse for allowing violence against Native people, especially Native women and children. Congress needs to act as quickly as possible to afford Alaskan Native Tribes and Villages the right to control crime in their own communities and include within that action the repeal of Section 910 of the Violence Against Women Reauthorization Act of 2013.

Funding in P.L. 280 States and for Alaska Efforts

While the safety of Native persons should never be based upon monetary considerations, and every federally recognized tribe should be afforded the right to exercise its inherent sovereign authority to protect its people and its lands, until we can secure a substantial increase in the federal dollars available to pay for these costs, available federal dollars have to be directed first to those areas which have no state police jurisdiction over Indian Crime. This is unfortunate, but it is just that simple.

Thank You

Again thank you for allowing us this opportunity to present our concerns. The GPTCA and its Member Tribes look forward to working closely with the Committee to address these critical issues.

PREPARED STATEMENT OF ELAINE D. WILLMAN, DIRECTOR, COMMUNITY
DEVELOPMENT AND TRIBAL AFFAIRS, VILLAGE OF HOBART

Specific to the *January 29, 2014 Letter of Recommendations* provided by the Indian Law &
Order Commission, the Village of Hobart submits comments for consideration by the Senate
Committee on Indian Affairs (SCIA), the Bureau of Indian Affairs (BIA), the Department of
Justice (DOJ), and various members of Congress.

OVERARCHING CONCERNS

1. Senators must give close scrutiny to the ILOC Recommendations as to whether
   recommendations comport with the U.S. Constitution;

2. Senators must be assured that the Senate Committee on Indian Affairs establishes
   panels for future Hearings on ILOC Recommendations that always include the voice
   of directly impacted local governments, non-tribal law enforcement officials and non-
   tribal residents;

3. Any implementation of DOJ-ILOC Recommendations must respect and ensure that
   tribal governments, nor tribal courts have authority over non-members. *(VAWA
   Domestic Abuse exception noted).*

We understand that crime upon remote, large land-based Indian reservations is a true
emergency, in need of significant increase in resources to make areas safe for Indian families.
Hobart officials and staff have reviewed the findings and recommendations of the Indian Law
and Order Commission (ILOC) and commend this Committee for its dedication, due diligence
and specificity of recommendations. Below are our comments in support of some
recommendations and opposition to others:

A SEPARATE INDIAN JUDICIARY SYSTEM

The first sentence of Article III, Section 1 of the U.S. Constitution states: *"The Judicial Power of
the United States, shall be vested in one supreme Court, and in such inferior Courts as the Congress
may from time to time ordain and establish."*

The implication that Congress can create a separate judiciary system that is ethnicity based, and
stands free and separate from courts previously established by Congress, is a premise entirely
inconsistent with the intent of Article III of the Constitution. A separate "Indian Judiciary" with
any authority over non-tribal citizens directly contravenes the Fourteen Amendment as well.

The ILOC recommendation letter reports that, "The (new and separate) 'Court of Indian Appeals" would be authorized to hear all appeals relating to alleged violation of the 4th (warrants/search/seizure), 5th (due process); 6th (speedy trial) and 8th (excessive bail, cruel, unusual punishment) Amendments of the United States Constitution..." The irony of this statement is that even the existence of such a separate, autonomous ethnicity-based judiciary automatically creates "violations" of the foregoing and other critical Constitutional Amendments for non-tribal citizens residing within or near former or existing Indian reservations.

By this letter, we remind our federal elected and federal administrative officials, and other readers to remember such IRA history, and not repeat it in the 21st century. The ILOC judiciary recommendations are less innovative and more surreptitious in resurrecting a whole section (Title IV) of the 1934 IRA that Congress long ago rendered unconstitutional. The effort to create a separate Indian judiciary is not new; it was first attempted by Commissioner John Collier within the original legislation of the 1934 Indian Reorganization Act (IRA) (H.R. 7902, 73rd Congress, 2nd Session, February 12, 1934). Title IV of John Collier's original IRA legislation was entitled "Court of Indian Appeals" and contained 25 sections that are once again encompassed in the ILOC Recommendations. In 1934 Congress recognized the fallacy and unconstitutionality of such a separate "Indian judicial system" and removed this entire section from the final IRA Act before its adoption on June 18, 1934 (48. Stat. 984).

STRENGTHENING TRIBAL JUSTICE

We certainly affirm the need for strengthening tribal justice on remote Indian reservations of predominantly Indian population. Even so, adjudicatory authority over non-members violates the fundamental rights of non-tribal U.S. citizens. The net effect of the recommendations of the ILOC that encourage further autonomy that erodes congressional and judicial oversight of these quasi-dependent sovereign governments goes head-on into conflict with Article II, Section 4 of the U.S. Constitution: *"New States may be admitted by the Congress into this Union; but no new State shall be formed or erected within the jurisdiction of any other State..."*

The municipality of Hobart, co-located within the boundaries of the former Oneida Indian reservation, has 7,100 population of which approximately 900 are enrolled Oneida Indians. All Hobart residents, including tribal members are within minutes from a district, state or federal court in nearby Green Bay, Wisconsin. Tribal members are full and individual U.S. citizens who can immediately access a local, state or federal elected official by phone, email or in person. Their submission/enrollment in a tribal government is a personal choice that does not deny them the same privileges as every other citizen in Wisconsin or this country. This scenario certainly applies to Indian tribes in metropolitan areas in the western states of Washington, Oregon, California, as well as the Great Lakes and New England states.

Already, with the adoption of the Violence Against Women Act (VAWA), a landmark ruling, *Oliphant v. Suquamish* (435 U.S. 191 (1978) has been penetrated, and perhaps rightfully so if VAWA is forever limited to domestic abuse incidents only. However, for 35 years, *Oliphant* has been the bright line set by the Rehnquist Court, based upon the U.S. Civil Rights Act of 1968 that denies tribal governments "inherent criminal jurisdiction" over non-tribal members. Any

Congressional act or administrative policy that erases the bright-line shield of *Oliphant* may well invite chaos on otherwise peaceful reservations that are predominantly non-Indian in population. The Juvenile Justice system should be no exception to the *Oliphant* rule.

Boundaries and jurisdiction are fundamental to the governing system of this country. It must be possible for co-located governments to mutually respect governing authority that is clearly defined, unclouded by overreaching federal power, or superior "sovereignties." The preservation of Public Law 280 ensures clarity and preserves a State's ability to protect its residents.

Currently in 2014 and the coming years, a rapidly growing voice of American citizenry is raising its concerns about the teetering imbalance of the three branches of federal government over Affordable Care Act, and other federal policies. It is an understatement to report that the overreaching of the Executive branch of government such as EPA, BIA, and DOJ is even more on the move with federal Indian policy overreaching that is spreading the footprint of federal jurisdiction and authority over lands within states.

Congress and the Senate Committee on Indian Affairs might well heed the voices and backlash when intentional erosion of state and citizen sovereignty, and diminishment of private property rights obtains from the implementation of federal Indian policy. When decisions are made absent the concerns of impacted local governments, conflict, costly and unnecessary litigation, and system failure is surely guaranteed.

At their meeting of March 4, 2014 the Board of Trustees of the Village of Hobart requested that I submit this letter on behalf of thousands of non-tribal residents in Hobart likely to be significantly and negatively impacted by any of the ILOC recommendations of January 29, 2014.

RESPONSE TO WRITTEN QUESTIONS SUBMITTED BY HON. TIM JOHNSON TO TROY A. EID AND AFFIE ELLIS

Question. On the topic of juvenile justice, what methods of rehabilitation for Native juvenile offenders have been most effective? What preventative measures can be taken to lower the incarceration rate of Native youth?

Answer. Of foremost importance in the treatment and rehabilitation of Native youth is bringing the juveniles into a community-based treatment rather than detention in distant locations. Assessment, treatment and other services that attend to juvenile trauma should be local, fully integrated with tribal child welfare and local behavioral health agencies. It is only at the local, tribal level that tribal elders can play a role in mentoring, instructing and healing juveniles. The most positive rehabilitation outcomes have been where there is continuity of culture, community support and events, and integration with prevention programs.

The Commission visited the Rosebud Sioux Reservation in South Dakota in May 2012 and learned about the tribe's effort to educate juvenile offenders and not just incarcerate them. The Commission met Miskoo Petite, Facility Administrator for the Wanbli Wiconi Tipi, a juvenile detention center, and visited the center to learn about its services. The center conducts a Juvenile Assessment and Intervention system for each juvenile, weaving together a risk and needs assessment. The center provides moral reconation therapy designed to bolster ego, social, moral and positive behavioral growth. The center has group discussion about gang prevention, suicide prevention, anti-bullying and other behavior management strategies. The center requires daily exercise, offers an educational program, including Lakota language and cultural classes, and provides voluntary prayer circles and sweat lodge sessions. Petite testified that when young people have their basic needs met, they perform better academically.

Additionally, the Commission learned about center's Green Re-entry program, supported by a federal Office of Juvenile Justice Delinquency Prevention grant that provided resources to allow juveniles to develop and implement environmentally green technologies. Specifically, juveniles receive education and training opportunities to create organic gardens, bee keeping, biodiesel fuels and renewable energy in solar and wind energy. Rosebud Children's Court Judge Janel Sully testified about the program and stated, "When the youth come in they are sullen, angry and upset.

They spend some time in the Green Entry program and in a matter of days they are smiling, happy and energetic.''

Other effective preventive programs have been local youth councils programs, such as the UNITY chapter at Wind River Reservation, the Boys and Girls Clubs, such as at the Pine Ridge Reservation, and integration into community sports teams, active social services, anti-bullying programs and education on the effects of drug and alcohol abuse. The Boys and Girls Clubs of America, when integrated into reservation life and when appropriately funded, have made a significant difference in establishing role models for juveniles, keeping them away from drugs and alcohol, bringing them into contact with a continuous line of mentors and past graduates of the tribally-based club, and serving as a ''home away from home,'' especially for those juveniles from broken and dysfunctional homes or abusive families.

RESPONSE TO WRITTEN QUESTIONS SUBMITTED BY HON. MARK BEGICH TO TROY A. EID AND AFFIE ELLIS

Question 1. Can you further explain the report's finding in Chapter 2 that ''the State of Alaska cannot simultaneously assert that, outside the Metlakatla Reservation, there is no Indian country in Alaska and that P.L. 83–280 prevails.'' This is a concept that has not received much public discussion.

Answer. Public Law 83–280 by its terms only authorizes state jurisdiction within ''Indian country.'' See 18 U.S.C. Sec. 1162; 28 U.S.C. Sec. 1360. Therefore, if the State of Alaska is denying that Indian country exists outside the Metlakatla Reservation, it must also be denying that state jurisdiction is authorized on those lands under P.L. 83–280. State jurisdiction may exist on those lands for other reasons, but not because of P.L. 83–280.

Question 2. In Chapter 2, the report suggests that in order to ''avoid ongoing and costly litigation, State-Tribal relations should be characterized by respect, mutual recognition, and partnership.''

Answer. The Commission's unanimous position is that State-Tribal relations in Alaska and the rest of our country should be based on mutual recognition and respect. *See Roadmap for Making Native America Safer,* Ch. 2, pg. 47. Unfortunately, the State of Alaska instead tends to favor legal and policy positions that marginalize the potential for Alaska Native Nations to make and enforce their own criminal laws to prevent, deter and punish violent crime. The enclosed essay by Chairman Eid from *Alaska Dispatch News,* dated June 21, 2014, highlights some of the Commission's findings and recommendations on these important issues.

The Commission respectfully encourages Governor Parnell and his administration to reassess their current preference for litigating with Alaska Native Nations instead of cooperating more closely with them. Alaska Natives, after all, are also Alaska state citizens. Seemingly open-ended litigation over these issues by the State of Alaska, the Commission noted in its report, undermines public safety. It makes it more rather than less difficult for different jurisdictions to work together to protect lives and property. In the lower 48, where tribes and local governments frequently set aside their differences and enter into inter-governmental agreements for criminal justice—in many cases, simply ''agreeing to disagree'' and setting aside the jurisdictional questions for another day—the two sovereigns have made substantial progress in interdicting crime, making arrests, and bringing offenders to justice. The result is increased confidence in criminal justice overall, the real benefit of crime deterrence, and increased support for the victims of crime. Alaska is currently on the wrong path, but it does not have to be this way.

Question 3. The State of Alaska's current approach to solve these issues, as was noted in the report, has been to increase funding for VPSOs. In addition to this, the State has also launched a public campaign known as Choose Respect. Once a year communities across Alaska and in Washington D.C. rally in an effort to raise awareness about domestic violence issues. In your time in Alaska, did you identify tangible results from either of these efforts?

Answer. While the Alaska Attorney General made mention of the Governor's ''Choose Respect'' Initiative in his February 1, 2013 letter to the Commission, the Commission itself did not see or hear of any change in the reports of domestic violence or sexual assault in Alaska Native communities as a result of the initiative. Raising awareness about domestic violence is certainly a worthy goal, particularly given that reported rates of domestic violence in Alaska are as high as 10 times the national average, according to the Commission's report.

Question 3a. Do you think that the Governor's ''Choose Respect'' campaign does anything to strengthen 'State-Tribal' relations? What could work better?

Answer. Without knowing of any tangible result of the campaign, beyond the youth rallies and marches, the Commission is unable to speculate on its potential for success. It is clearly a worthwhile and laudable goal, and the Commission supports that goal wholeheartedly. Yet according to the most recent Legislative Report on the "Choose Respect" campaign, the campaign itself does not appear to include any direct outreach to or partnership with Alaska Native Nations. While the campaign would increase VSPO numbers and data collection, it relies almost exclusively on existing state agencies and community non-profit entities to implement its programs and channel its expenditures. In sum, the campaign is aimed at promoting public awareness, which is a good and worthwhile objective, but does little to "strengthen 'State-Tribal' relations'" because the State still refuses to recognize and respect Alaska Native Nations on a government-to-government basis.

The Governor's office should consider consulting with tribal governments to discuss ways that the campaign can channel expenditures, program assets and goals, and overall efforts to the tribal government entities that can implement locally-based preventive programs, education, wrap-around services, and increased enforcement and prosecution. The campaign should also encourage appropriate inter-governmental agreements with Alaska Native tribal councils to jointly implement some of the campaign elements on a government-to-government basis with the State of Alaska—sharing resources, accountability and responsibility.

Question 4. In your opinion, would arming Village Police Safety Officers with guns enhance village public safety?

Answer. Arming VPSOs would enhance not only Village public safety, but the safety of the VPSOs themselves. Alcohol and controlled substances are associated with a high proportion of offenses committed in Alaska Native communities, and many households and offenders already possess firearms. This volatile combination makes it very risky for law enforcement officers to respond to calls for service.

The two VPSOs killed in the line of duty (Thomas Madole on 3–19–2013 and Ronald Zimin on 10–22–1986) were killed by gunfire. Both VPSOs are honored on the National Law Enforcement Memorial in Washington, DC. This pattern of officer deaths is hardly unique to Alaska Native Villages. Three-quarters of all law enforcement officers killed in the line of duty in Alaska were killed by gunfire.

Both houses of the Alaska legislature recently voted to have VPSOs be armed, and this legislation has been sent to the Governor for his signature. The Indian Law and Order Commission strongly supports this legislation. The bill sponsor's statement puts it well: "VPSOs work often without backup in remote locations where a call to the State Troopers can mean hours before backup arrives. I believe my fellow legislators will agree that it is not reasonable to continue to ask our VPSOs to walk unarmed into situations that pose obvious dangers. It's my hope that arming these first responders will have a deterrent effect that makes not just the officers but whole communities safer."

Question 5. Are you aware of any existing models that have been successful in banning or limiting the importation of alcohol/drugs in populations seeking to reduce crime related to alcohol, which Alaska can look to as an option to address this problem?

Answer. Best practices in this area appear to be lacking. The experience to date suggests that tribal laws banning or limiting alcohol possession, distribution and "bootlegging" are only as good as their practical enforcement, which is often severely deficient. Native Nations in the lower 48 have the option under 18 U.S.C. § 1161 to opt-out of federal liquor control laws applicable to Indian country. Consequently, some Indian reservations are considered "dry," because sale and/or possession of alcohol is prohibited under federal and tribal law, while others allow possession and/or sale of alcohol. Although the causal relationship is unclear, there is no evidence that tribes prohibiting possession and/or sale of alcohol experience lower levels of substance abuse and crime. Moreover, where alcohol is prohibited on reservations, nearby offreservation communities often become places where reservation residents congregate to purchase and abuse alcohol, making local roads dangerous. Thus, the Indian Law and Order Commission did not recommend reintroducing federal laws that would ban all introduction of alcohol onto reservations.

With respect to Alaska, the Commission found evidence that illegal shipments of alcohol and controlled substances are having extremely harmful effects in Alaska Native communities, and federal and state officials are largely ineffective in stopping such traffic. For example, the Captain of the North Slope Borough Police Department explained how bootlegging and illegal drugs are the scourge of Barrow, where alcohol can be imported, subject to supposedly strict regulations and restrictions. Most alcohol comes in through the U.S. Postal Service at the local post office, and in air charters, which do not have inspections, examinations, or dog sniffers (or metal detectors, no less backscatter X-ray machines). People are flying in and out of Barrow all day long (weather permitting) with boxes, bags and containers. Sexual assaults are frequently the result of binges with the alcohol smuggled in, consumed without limit, with the victims often unconscious or heavily intoxicated during the attacks. More enforcement resources are definitely needed to intercept and seize illegal shipments of alcohol and controlled substances, along with building Alaska Native tribal capacity to control alcohol and drug abuse at the local level.

The Commission stands ready to continue working with the Committee to implement the recommendations of the *Roadmap*. It is imperative that we continue to work together to make Native American and Alaska Native Nations safer and more just for all U.S. citizens. Your leadership and that of your colleagues is making a positive difference and is greatly appreciated by all of us in the field. Please let us know how we can be of continued service.

Attachment

ALASKA DISPATCH NEWS (HTTP://WWW.ALASKADISPATCH.COM)—TROY A. EID—JUNE 21, 2014

OPINION: We members of the Indian Law and Order Commission keep returning to Alaska because we're convinced that the lack of accountability for criminals who keep harming women and children in rural and urban Alaska is something Alaskans can and will fix.

Entering a taxi cab at the Ted Stevens Airport, the driver asks: "How much longer are you going to keep coming to Alaska?" A cabbie in Fairbanks said the same thing to me last March.

It's refreshing how many Alaskans have heard about the Indian Law and Order Commission and its recent report urging the State of Alaska, the Federal Government, and all 229 Alaska Native Nations to work together to make Alaska safer and more just.

The report of the all-volunteer, bi-partisan commission, "A Roadmap for Making Native America Safer," highlights Alaska's violent crime epidemic. This includes a domestic violence rate 10 times the national average and sexual assault rates 12 times higher. It's a crisis in the Bush, but also in Anchorage and other cities where families flee when village life becomes unbearable. Where criminals keep victimizing women and children because they were never held accountable for their crimes back home.

My fellow commissioners and I keep coming back because we're convinced this lack of accountability is something Alaskans can and will fix.

Admittedly, the commission's report concluded that Alaska's current policy is on the wrong track. Many State policies marginalize the potential of Alaska Native Nations to prevent and combat crime in their own communities.

Instead of respecting Tribally based sovereignty and self-government as other states routinely do, Alaska tries to police and judge Native citizens from afar using too few people and resources: Colonialism on the cheap.

If we've learned anything from the Big Government policy failures of the 1960s and 1970s, it's that federal and state leaders must help locally elected governments build their own crime-fighting and prevention efforts, not the other way around. Crime control strategies need to be locally tailored and enforced—and court decisions given full faith and credit by the State—to be effective. Yet precisely the opposite often happens in Alaska, which has the nation's most centralized law enforcement system. The commission found, for example, that in 75 Alaska Native Nations, the State asserts exclusive criminal jurisdiction but routinely provides no law enforcement services at all.

Elsewhere there aren't enough Village Public Safety Officers (VPSOs) and other first responders on the ground. The lack of basic infrastructure supporting them in the bush is inexplicable. It's been more than a half-century since statehood, yet there's just one women's shelter in any Alaska Native village and no shelters where children can escape their perpetrators.

Nor should Alaska Troopers—among the finest public servants anywhere—be fairly expected to work miracles from afar. When the commission visited the Village of Tanana in October 2012, the Tribal Council told us someone would probably get killed there unless the State helped them boost the capacity of the Village's court system and supported local policing and family protective services. As we talked that day, a repeat violent offender freely roamed Tanana's streets despite Tribal court restraining orders against him, orders the State refused to recognize.

The tribal leaders with whom we met in Tanana and many other villages demanded swift State action so they could do more to help themselves. They wanted recognition and respect, not a handout. They need Tribally based police and courts with the capacity to enforce the civil rights of all Alaskans, Native and non-Native alike.

This same approach already works well in much of the Lower 48, which is why Congress last year recognized Tribal court jurisdiction there by enacting the Violence Against Women Act (VAWA). VAWA permits Native Nations to enforce laws criminalizing domestic violence over all citizens with Tribes' territories so long as their courts enforce defendants' constitutional rights.

This is the same Tanana where Seargent Scott Johnson and Trooper Gabe Rich were brutally murdered in Tanana last May 1st while responding to an earlier threat against an unarmed VPSO. In the same state where violence in many villages has decimated the citizenry so that average life expectancies are closer to Haiti's than the rest of the United States.

So why are we so bullish that times are changing for the better for Alaska Natives and indeed all Alaskans?

It isn't just a growing awareness of the problem, necessary though that is. Plenty of Alaskans, including those who email me daily, are saying that enough is enough.

This past February, Alaska's senior U.S. Senator, Lisa Murkowski—who co-sponsored VAWA—declared it now needs to be extended to Alaska Native Nations. Both Alaska's Senators are now vowing to make that happen.

This could be a watershed. Recognizing Alaska Native Nations' power over all citizens to bring perpetrators of domestic violence to justice will, over time, confirm and accelerate the larger trend in Alaska and across the country to help Native Nations make and enforce their own laws. Where that's already happened elsewhere, the commission documented that violent crime rates have gone down. The same can happen in Alaska.

In recent years, the State has insisted that Alaska Native Nations lack any territorial sovereignty, or legal control over their lands—a conclusion contradicted by Federal law, as the commission's report and previous studies by Alaska's own experts make clear. Extending VAWA to Alaska, however, will make it essential for the State and Alaska Native villages to determine jointly—on a government-to-government basis—the precise boundaries in which tribes' have civil and criminal jurisdiction to make and enforce their own domestic violence laws over Native and non-Native people living and working there.

This line-drawing can happen in many different ways—by negotiating inter-governmental agreements between Native Nations and the State, for example—and need not replicate the Indian reservation system in the Lower 48, as is sometimes mistakenly suggested.

Once territorial lines are drawn for VAWA purposes, they can be enforced not by State fiat or decree, but through a process of give-and-take based on mutual recognition and respect. Both sides will have a seat at the table. State policy will begin to shift toward building more Tribally based capacity for self-governance in order to keep the peace and respect everyone's civil rights.

Looking forward, as such jurisdictional lines are drawn between the State and Alaska Native Nations as VAWA requires, those same territorial boundaries can be used for other public safety purposes—to combat the scourage of drugs and alcohol and host of other ills plaguing the bush and radiating into the cities.

Thanks in part to VAWA, we believe a much brighter future may be replacing the old Colonial model and the violence it begets, a future worthy of Alaska's independent heritage and values. This future will be built the Alaska way—not imposed by outsiders. But it can and we believe will be accomplished.

It will be a privilege to keep coming back to Alaska and see how much you will keep achieving by working together.

———

RESPONSE TO WRITTEN QUESTIONS SUBMITTED BY HON. HEIDI HEITKAMP TO HON. TIMOTHY Q. PURDON

Question 1. In my state of North Dakota, there are high levels of repeat offenders involved in substance abuse-related offenses. On the Standing Rock Indian Reservation, according to a recent survey:

- Alcohol is a factor in 80-percent of all criminal arrests—a rate over 220 percent that of the DOJ's statistical average.
- In arrests where alcohol is a factor, the average alcohol level at the time of booking was over 310 percent of the legal limit; while 1 in 5 register potentially fatal levels.
- 39 percent of the adults on the reservation are booked annually for a substance abuse related offense.

• Nearly half of those individuals were arrested at least one more time within the calendar year—again for a substance abuse offense.

Rather than just treating the problem, we need to treat the source by addressing underlying substance abuse issues in order to reduce recidivism rates.

What steps have been taken to promote reentry programs in tribal communities to combat recidivism?

Answer. Incarceration is not the answer in every criminal case. Across the nation, at least 17 states have shifted resources away from prison construction in favor of treatment and supervision as a better means of reducing recidivism. The Attorney General is encouraging the United States Attorney's Offices to help reduce recidivism through various alternatives. In appropriate instances involving non-violent offenses, prosecutors are encouraged to consider alternatives to incarceration, such as drug courts, specialty courts, or other diversion programs. Accordingly, the Department will soon issue a "best practices" memorandum to U.S. Attorney Offices, including those offices with Indian Country responsibilities, encouraging more widespread adoption of these diversion policies when appropriate.

In its memorandum, the Department will endorse certain existing diversion programs as models. For example, in the Central District of California, the United States Attorney's Offices (USAO), the court, the Federal Public Defender, and the Pretrial Services Agency (PSA) have together created a two-track specialty court/post-plea diversion program, known as the Conviction and Sentence Alternatives (CASA) program. Selection for the program is not made solely by the USAO, but by the program team, comprised of the USAO, the Public Defender, PSA, and the court. Track one is for candidates with minimal criminal histories whose criminal conduct appears to be an aberration that could appropriately be addressed by supervision, restitution and community service. Examples of potential defendants include those charged with felony, though relatively minor, credit card or benefit fraud, mail theft, and narcotics offenses. Track two is for those defendants with somewhat more serious criminal histories whose conduct appears motivated by substance abuse issues. Supervision in these cases includes intensive drug treatment. Examples of eligible defendants are those charged with non-violent bank robberies, or mail and credit card theft designed to support a drug habit.

The Department will also recommend the use of specialty courts and programs to deal with unique populations. Examples include a treatment court for veterans charged with misdemeanors in the Western District of Virginia, and the Federal/Tribal Pretrial Diversion program in the District of South Dakota, which is designed specifically for juvenile offenders in Indian country.

To lead these efforts on a local level, the Department is establishing a prevention and reentry coordinator within each of the USAO's, including in Indian country, to focus on prevention and reentry efforts. As part of this enhanced commitment, Assistant U.S. Attorneys (AUSA) will be encouraged to devote time to reentry issues in addition to casework. The Executive Office of U.S. Attorneys will report periodically on the progress made in USAOs on this program.

In addition, the Department of Justice's Bureau of Justice Assistance (BJA) offers grant resources and training and technical assistance to tribes and tribal justice systems to support effective interventions for drug involved offenders. This includes funding to support planning, interventions, enforcement and prevention resources through its Coordinated Tribal Assistance Solicitation (CTAS) in purpose areas 2 and 3. This includes the use of a healing to wellness court model, a drug court model developed specifically for tribal justice systems; prevention and treatment programming for those in the tribal justice system; and effective supervision in the community through the creation and enhancement of tribal probation agencies.

Other efforts to aid reentry are also being launched. The consequences of a criminal conviction can remain long after someone has served his or her sentence. Rules and regulations pertaining to formerly incarcerated people can limit employment and travel opportunities, making a proper transition back into society difficult. The Department worked with the American Bar Association to publish a catalogue of these collateral consequences imposed at the state and federal level. To address these barriers to reentry, the Attorney General issued a new memorandum to Department of Justice components, requiring them to factor these collateral consequences into their rulemaking. If the rules imposing collateral consequences are found to be unduly burdensome and not serving a public safety purpose, they should be narrowly tailored or eliminated.

The Attorney General's Interagency Reentry Council has published helpful materials on reentry efforts related to employment, housing, and parental rights. In an update to these materials, the Department will publish new fact sheets on ways to reduce unnecessary barriers to reentry in two areas: (1) to connect the reentering population with legal services to address obstacles such as fines and criminal records expungement when appropriate; and (2) to highlight efforts to reduce or eliminate fines at the local level.

BJA provides resources to support the reentry of tribal members from tribal jails as well as federal, Bureau of Indian Affairs (BIA) and state prisons. Under CTAS and the Second Chance Act funds, BJA has funded a number of tribes in building tribal reentry strategies, often in coordination with the U.S. Attorney or state Departments of Corrections. Recently, BJA issued a fact sheet that summarizes the resources available to tribes to support tribal reentry efforts as well as some promising practices. *https://www.bja.gov/Publications/TribalReentryFS.pdf* BJA is also working with other federal partners to launch a new training program for tribal and federal partners to support planning of strategies to support reentry of tribal members from federal and state prisons.

Question 2. Federal courts are often located many hours away from where crimes occur on Indian reservations. As a result, defendants and witnesses must be transported to federal court, which is time consuming and expensive. Tribal courts provide a local solution to tribal law and order issues yet, they often lack capacity. What can be done to strengthen tribal court systems?

Answer. The Department is dedicated to helping tribes enhance tribal self-governance, particularly through efforts to improve tribes' court systems. In that regard, the Office of Justice Programs (OJP), funds grants to promote crime fighting and public safety strategies and is committed to preventing and controlling crime, violence, and substance abuse and improving the functioning of criminal justice systems in American Indian and Alaska Native communities. OJP works closely with the tribes to help foster leadership, good management, and quality services in grant administration and policy development. OJP also coordinates with other U.S. Department of Justice components and other agencies and organizations to ensure that limited federal funds are used to achieve the maximum possible benefit. As part of CTAS purpose area 3, tribes can apply to BJA for a range of funding to support the creation and enhancement of tribal justice systems. In addition, BJA administers a wide array of training and technical assistance programs for tribal judges, prosecutors, defense counsel and court administrators. OJP works collaboratively with American Indian and Alaska Native officials to develop, implement, and enhance justice systems that reflect community values, needs, and expectations; and provides assistance to plan and construct tribal justice facilities including tribal jails, transitional housing, and multipurpose justice centers.

An additional way that the Department can help strengthen tribal courts is through the use of Tribal Special Assistant United States Attorneys (SAUSAs). Tribal SAUSAs are tribal prosecutors who are employees of a Tribe, but who are cross-designated as Special Assistant United States Attorneys. With the assistance of a full-time AUSA, SAUSAs can prosecute certain Indian Country cases in federal court. SAUSAs benefit from Department training at the National Advocacy Center, and the close working relationships that develop in a Tribal SAUSA program. In 2012, the Office on Violence Against Women (OVW) announced that four tribes in Nebraska, New Mexico, Montana, North Dakota and South Dakota were awarded cooperative agreements to cross-designate tribal prosecutors to pursue violence against women cases in both tribal and federal courts. Through this special initiative, OVW supports salary, travel, and training costs of four tribal SAUSAs, who will work in collaboration with the U.S. Attorneys Offices in the Districts of Nebraska, New Mexico, Montana, North Dakota, and South Dakota. These prosecutors maintain an active violence against women crimes caseload, in tribal and/or federal court, while also helping to promote higher quality investigations, improved training, and better inter-governmental communication.

To better understand the capacity, needs and challenges faced by tribal court systems, several major projects are underway to help the Department gather needed data to respond effectively for long term solutions. In FY 2014, the Bureau of Justice Statistics (BJS) continued the development of the 2014 National Survey of Tribal Court Systems (NSTCS). The NSTCS will be BJS's first statistical collection focusing on tribal justice systems since 2002. Through the NSTCS, BJS will gather vital information on the administrative and operational characteristics of tribal justice systems (including budgets, staffing, caseloads and case processes), indigent defense services, tribal-state joint jurisdiction courts, pretrial and probation programs, reentry programs, protection orders and domestic violence, and juvenile cases; implementation of various enhanced sentencing provisions of the Tribal Law and Order Act (TLOA); and various indigenous or traditional dispute forums operating within Indian country. The NSTCS will be sent to all 566 federally recognized tribes, including those with known tribal justice systems and those with unknown judicial forums, as well as the Courts of Federal Regulations. This project was recently announced in the Federal Register in March 2014.

Additionally, the Office of Sex Offender Sentencing, Monitoring, Apprehending, Registering and Tracking (SMART) works with 165 Federally Recognized tribes to implement the Sex Offender Registration and Notification Act (SORNA). The SORNA implementing tribes that have courts cooperate in the formation of these registries including adapting new tribal codes, enactment and enforcement of failure to register penalties and other essential functions in the registering, notification and management of sex offenders. The SMART Office has provided funding to many of these tribe to help their courts build infrastructure that not only contributes to their sex offender registration programs but enhances their criminal justice systems on a broader basis.

Question 3. The Mandan Hidatsa and Arikara Nation is in the middle of an unprecedented growth as a result of the oil boom in the Bakken Formation. The influx of new people in the region has attracted high crime, placing great strain on state, local, and tribal resources available to respond. It has also highlighted the need for greater cooperation between all three entities to combat crime. The *Roadmap* recommends embracing intergovernmental cooperation and coordination as a solution to the jurisdictional issues which tribes and states face when policing large areas. What is being done to promote Memorandums of Understanding between tribes and states? Specifically, what is the Attorney General doing to incentivize state and local governments to work closer with tribes?

Answer. Section 222 of the Tribal Law and Order Act of 2010 provides that the Attorney General "may provide technical and other assistance to State, tribal, and local governments that enter into cooperative agreements, including agreements relating to mutual aid, hot pursuit of suspects, and cross-deputization for the purposes of—

(1) Improving law enforcement effectiveness;
(2) Reducing crime in Indian country and nearby communities; and
(3) Developing successful cooperative relationships that effectively combat crime in Indian country and nearby communities.''

The DOJ COPS Office funded the creation of a training curriculum and technical assistance effort that focuses on collaboration among tribal and local law enforcement, including the development ofMOUs/MOAs/Cross-Deputizations that is provided by the Western Community Policing Institute (WCPI). Through this program, now funded by BJA, WCPI offers regional trainings that focus on building effective and efficient collaborative law enforcement partnerships throughout Indian Country to address the unique public safety threats to tribal communities and their neighboring jurisdictions. The training curriculum includes understanding cultural diversity issues, identifying stakeholders, the need for regional collaboration, and how to develop effective memoranda of understandings and agreements. In addition, COPS has a library of resources available to assist tribes and other stakeholders in developing and sustaining regional community policing partnerships.

The COPS Office also has a Tribal Public Law 280 Policing Partnerships project that is in development. To strengthen the relationship between tribal law enforcement, non-tribal law enforcement, and U.S./States Attorneys in Public Law 280 sites, Strategic Applications International (SAI) will leverage its vast experience in facilitating strategy and action planning summits to address crime, drugs, and other social issues in partnership with law enforcement and key stakeholders, together with their experience in working with tribal law enforcement. The program will include approximately four sites where a two-day site specific Community Oriented Policing Training augmented with cultural dialogue training and action planning will be delivered. Participants will include Sheriffs, Chiefs of Police, U.S. Attorneys, and Tribal Leaders. The results of the on-site technical assistance will aid in the development of a web-based training curriculum tailored to Public Law 280 communities to enhance tribal and non-tribal law enforcement cooperation. The program goal is to improve public safety on tribal lands by developing a training program that builds the knowledge, skills and abilities of tribal law enforcement agencies to build more effective relationships with non-tribal law enforcement to advance community policing. This project is in its initial stages as the four on-site locations are selected and training and technical assistance begins.

BJA also has a robust portfolio of training and technical assistance to support intergovernmental collaboration agreements. Working with the Tribal Law and Policy Institute, BJA is sponsoring state-tribal court forums and meetings to support interagency collaboration agreements, meetings and sharing of codes and resource materials. BJA also sponsors the "Walking on Common Ground" Web Site *(www.WalkingOnCommonGround.org)* that serves as an ongoing comprehensive resource highlighting promising practices in tribal/state court collaboration and providing resource toolkits for those wishing to replicate such practices. This site provides extensive information and resources concerning tribal/state/federal court collaboration and encourages intergovernmental collaboration and cooperation. BJA is also working with the Oregon Health and Science University to support the promotion of the joint jurisdiction court model. COPS is also working with the National Sheriff's Association on the initial stages of a project to develop model cross-deputization agreements. Finally, DOJ works with tribal and local partners on specific MOUs when requested to do so.

The rapid development in the Bakken Region caused by the oil boom has resulted in substantial strain upon the residents of the surrounding areas, including the Fort Berthold Indian Reservation (Fort Berthold). The United States Attorney for North Dakota also recently noted a significant increase in the number of sexual assault cases that have been referred to that office for criminal prosecution. In response to this great need, the Department's Office for Victims of Crime has partnered with the Bureau of Indian Affairs to expand its National Victim Assistance Program by hiring a full-time Victim Specialist that will be based at Fort Berthold. This dedicated staff member will work with federal, state, local, and tribal officials to meet the needs of victims of crime at Fort Berthold and support local efforts to create a greater sense of safety and security among the residents of the reservation.

OVW is launching a special initiative to address violence against women, including sexual and domestic violence and stalking, within the Bakken region. OVW will support two specific components which comprise this initiative: (1) Enhanced Response to Victims, and (2) Tribal Special Assistant U.S. Attorneys.

The OVW Violence Against Women Bakken Region Initiative: Enhanced Response to Victims will support projects that are designed to address the unique challenges faced by victims, responders, and serve providers within this rural region, including challenges of geographic isolation, transportation barriers, economic structure, high cost of living, homelessness, and other social and cultural pressures. OVW encourages applicants to implement innovative approaches, through capacity-building and partnerships, to address the critical needs of victims in this region. Eligible applicants for this part of the initiative are:

- First Nations Women's Alliance in North Dakota
- Assiniboine and Sioux Tribes of the Fort Peck Indian Reservation in Montana
- The North Dakota Council on Abused Women's Services
- The Montana Coalition Against Domestic and Sexual Violence
- Three Affiliated Tribes of the Fort Berthold Reservation North Dakota

Through the Tribal Special Assistant U.S. Attorneys (Tribal SAUSAs) part of the initiative, OVW will support two Tribal SAUSAs to address the increased rise of violence against women on Indian reservations in Eastern Montana and Western North Dakota, in collaboration with the U.S. Attorney's Offices (USAOs) in those states. OVW will award grants to two tribes, selecting qualified applicants approved by participating USAOs. These cross-designated prosecutors will maintain an active violence against women crimes caseload, in tribal and/or federal court, while also helping to promote higher quality investigations, improved training, and better intergovernmental communication. These two awards are intended to increase the successful prosecution of domestic violence, dating violence, sexual assault and stalking in Indian country affected by the population boom in the Bakken region. Eligible tribes for SAUSAs are:

- Assiniboine and Sioux Tribes of the Fort Peck Indian Reservation in Montana
- Three Affiliated Tribes of the Fort Berthold Indian Reservation in North Dakota

The Mandan, Hidatsa and Arikara Nation (Three Affiliated Tribes) are working on implementing the Sex Offender Registration and Notification Act (SORNA) and has received training and technical assistance as well as grant funding from the Office of Sex Offender Sentencing, Monitoring, Apprehending, Registering and Tracking (SMART) to help the Tribes to build, implement and manage a sex offender registration and notification program. SORNA authorized implementing tribes including Three Affiliated to register a convicted sex offender (Native American or not) who lives, works or goes to school on Tribal land. It further created a federal violation for convicted offenders who fail to register; violations can be enforced by the U.S. Marshall Service (USMS) with the cooperation of the Tribes' registry office. Work on implementing a sex offender registration and notification program involves enhancement of tribal criminal justice infrastructure, information sharing, and collaboration with state, local and federal law enforcement. The Tribes have utilized the Tribe and Territory Sex Offender Registry System (TTSORS) provided by the SMART Office to set up a sex offender registry and public website which is linked to the National Sex Offender Public Website (NSOPW). At this writing, the Tribes have 35 sex offenders registered and publically posted on their website. The Tribes manage by their sex offender registration program, which is available to the public to help enhance public safety.

Question 4. Last year, Congress reauthorized the Violence Against Women Act which included an important provision expanding tribal sentencing and jurisdiction. What assistance is available to help large land based tribes and other tribes with limited resources to implement these important reforms?

Answer. In the Violence Against Women Act Reauthorization of 2013 (VAWA 2013), Congress authorized up to $25 million total for tribal grants in fiscal years 2014 to 2018, but Congress has not yet appropriated any of those funds. However, tribes may continue to apply for funding through the Department's Coordinated Tribal Assistance Solicitation (CTAS), which can support VA WA 2013 implementation. CTAS includes most of the tribal programs from the Department's Office of Justice Programs, Office of Community Oriented Policing Services (COPS), and the Office on Violence Against Women. In particular, tribes can apply under Purpose Area 3 for tribal justice systems and can apply under Purpose Area 5 for responses to violence against women. The programs served I 0 purpose areas and tribes were able to submit a single application while selecting multiple purpose areas, ranging from juvenile justice to violence against women.

Following the passage of VAWA 2013, the Department initiated and encouraged tribes to join the Intertribal Technical-Assistance Working Group (ITWG) on Special Domestic Violence Criminal Jurisdiction (SDVCJ). This peer-to-peer group allows tribes to exchange views, information, and advice about how tribes can best exercise SDVCJ, combat domestic violence, recognize victims' rights and safety needs, and fully protect defendants' rights. Tribes participating in the ITWG also have an opportunity to engage with the Departments of Justice and the Interior and to receive technical advice on specific issues or concerns as needed. The Department supports the ITWG with training and technical assistance to the extent possible with available resources. Participation in the ITWG is completely voluntary and not a prerequisite for tribes seeking to implement SDVCJ.

To complement these resources, BJA is also sponsoring training and technical assistance to the tribes seeking to implement the new authorization. BJA is also sponsoring training and technical assistance, including webinars and publications, on strategies to support tribes seeking to implement the enhanced sentencing authority under the Tribal Law and Order Act. This includes implementation of a number of the same requirements for implementation of this new domestic violence authority, as well as training for tribal probation and corrections on incarcerating and supervising these high risk offenders.

The Office on Violence Against Women currently administers 21 grant programs authorized by the *Violence Against Women Act of 1994* and subsequent legislation. These grant programs are designed to continue to develop the nation's capacity to reduce domestic violence, dating violence, sexual assault, and stalking by strengthening services to victims and holding offenders accountable for their actions. Presently four of these programs are targeted to Native American populations and tribes and are detailed within this section.

The Tribal Domestic Violence and Sexual Assault Coalitions Grant Program (Tribal Coalitions Program), authorized in the *Violence Against Women Act of 2000* (VAWA 2000), builds the capacity of survivors, advocates, Indian women's organizations, and victim service providers to form nonprofit, nongovernmental tribal domestic violence and sexual assault coalitions to end violence against American Indian and Alaska Native women. OVW's Tribal Coalitions Program grants are used to: increase awareness of domestic violence and sexual assault against American Indian and Alaska Native women; enhance the response to violence against women at the tribal, federal, and state levels; and identify and provide technical assistance to coalition membership and tribal communities to enhance access to essential services.

The Tribal Governments Program provides resources to: decrease the number of violent crimes committed against Indian women; help Indian tribes use their independent authority to respond to crimes of violence against Indian women; and make sure that people who commit violent crimes against Indian women are held responsible for their actions. It is administered within the CTAS. In Fiscal Year 2014, it was Purpose Area 5 of the CTAS.

The Sexual Assault Services Act has two funding streams that support tribes: the Tribal Sexual Assault Services Program, which provides funding for direct sexual assault victim services; and the Sexual Assault Services Program Grants to Tribal Coalitions, which supports tribal sexual assault coalitions.

The landmark American Recovery and Reinvestment Act of 2009 (Recovery Act), signed into law by President Obama, provided OVW with $20.8 million for the Indian Tribal Governments Program. The Recovery Act provided OVW with $2.8 million for the Tribal Domestic Violence and Sexual Assault Coalitions Program to provide much needed resources for organizing and supporting efforts to end violence against Indian women and provide technical assistance to member programs.

Question 5. As tribes begin to implement expanded jurisdictional authority under the Violence Against Women Act, there will likely be legal challenges. How is the Attorney General preparing to defend that jurisdiction without jeopardizing federal support and resources to tribes?

Answer. Since the Supreme Court's 1978 opinion in *Oliphant v. Suquamish Indian Tribe,* tribes have been prohibited from exercising criminal jurisdiction over non-Indian defendants. This included domestic violence and dating violence committed by non-Indian abusers against their Indian spouses, intimate partners, and dating partners. Even a violent crime committed by a non-Indian husband against his Indian wife, in the presence of her Indian children, in their home on the Indian reservation, could not be prosecuted by the tribe. In granting the pilot-project requests of the Pascua Yaqui, Tulalip, and Umatilla tribes, the United States is recognizing and affirming the tribes' inherent power to exercise ''special domestic violence criminal jurisdiction'' (SDVCJ) over all persons, regardless of their Indian or non-Indian status, for crimes committed on or after Feb. 20, 2014.

As described in the Department of Justice's Final Notice on the pilot project, the decisions are based on a diligent, detailed review of application questionnaires submitted by the tribes in December 2013, along with excerpts of tribal laws, rules, and policies, and other relevant information. That review, conducted in close coordination with the Department of the Interior and after formal consultation with affected Indian tribes, led the Justice Department to determine that the criminal justice systems of the Pascua Yaqui, Umatilla, and Tulalip tribes have adequate safeguards in place to fully protect defendants' rights under the Indian Civil Rights Act of 1968, as amended by VA WA 2013.

The Department of Justice posted notices of the pilot-project designation on its website and in the Federal Register. In addition, each tribe's application questionnaire and related tribal laws, rules, and policies will be posted on the Web site. These materials will serve as a resource for those tribes that may also wish to participate in the pilot project or to commence exercising SDVCJ in March 2015 or later, after the pilot project has concluded.

Question 6. In North Dakota, there are no juvenile justice facilities available to house juvenile offenders. The closest place a child can be taken right now is Lower Brule, South Dakota. For families who live on the Turtle Mountain Reservation, that is a 10 hour drive one way. Transporting children 10 hours away puts a great strain on families, and is a waste of very limited time and resources which could be better spent developing local solutions with better outcomes.

One solution is to develop alternatives to incarceration to reduce the need for such facilities. The *Roadmap* found rehabilitation through community service in a local community is more likely to prevent recidivism and therefore suggests funding for juvenile diversion programs to rehabilitate youth offenders. What is the Attorney General doing to assist tribes with developing juvenile diversion programs to keep children out of federal detention?

Answer. As mentioned in question one, the Department is working to publish a memorandum directing the use of alternative disposition short of incarceration. The incarceration of juveniles is particularly difficult and very disruptive to the community.

To assist the tribes dealing with juvenile diversion programs, the Department will recommend the use of specialty courts and programs to deal with unique populations. Examples include the Federal/Tribal Pretrial Diversion program in the District of South Dakota, which is designed specifically for juvenile offenders in Indian country. The district coordinates with the U.S. Probation Office, tribal prosecutors, and tribal courts to focus federal resources on the rehabilitative needs of juveniles in Indian country.

To lead these efforts on a local level, the Department is calling for U.S. Attorneys to designate a prevention and reentry coordinator within each of their offices to focus on prevention and reentry efforts. As part of this enhanced commitment, Assistant U.S. Attorneys will be encouraged to devote time to reentry issues in addition to casework. The Executive Office of U.S. Attorneys will report periodically on the progress made in USAOs on the reentry front.

In North Dakota, in the fall of 2012, the USAO launched a pilot program aimed at reaching young people on the Standing Rock Reservation. An AUSA in the office, who is himself an enrolled member in a North Dakota tribe, spearheaded the program. Since that time, he has organized a regular series of presentations to the student bodies of Standing Rock High School and Standing Rock Middle School designed to educate the students on protecting their personal safety and on the legal and physical/psychological hazards associated with certain conduct. The Standing Rock students have been receptive to these presentations, and we believe the program increased the students' trust in the law enforcement presenters.

Question 6a. I recognize some children with a history of violent crime may not be the best fit for participation in a diversion program. What is the Attorney General doing to develop juvenile detention space in North Dakota?

Answer. The Department agrees that few issues are more critical to the long-term improvement of public safety in Indian Country than working with young people to break the cycle of violence and hopelessness we have come to see on some reservations. Recognizing the importance of this issue, the Department is working to improve juvenile justice in Indian Country.

Federal juveniles are a special population with special designation needs. Each juvenile is placed in a facility that provides the appropriate level of programming and security. Several factors—such as age, offense, length of commitment, mental and physical health—are considered when making placements. Typically, federal juvenile offenders have committed violent offenses and have a history of responding to interventions and preventive measures in the community unfavorably. As a last resort, they are sentenced by the federal courts to the custody of the Bureau of Prisons (BOP).

The Department recognizes that treatment needs of the juvenile offender population must be continually monitored to ensure programs effectively meet existing needs. Juvenile offenders are placed at the most appropriate type of facility, which include the following: secure juvenile facilities that provide rehabilitation and accountability for federal juvenile offenders in a secure setting; and, non-secure juvenile facilities that, to achieve treatment and correctional objectives, provide rehabilitation and accountability for federal juvenile offenders by confining them in appropriate settings that allow offender access to and activities within the community under monitored conditions.

The BOP makes every effort to ensure the individual is prepared to manage that release successfully. The BOP attempts to place all federal juveniles close to home to facilitate community reintegration and their eventual reuniting with their families.

In fact, the process of family reunification begins during incarceration. In addition to encouraging family visitation, other services (e.g., individual and family counseling for juveniles, their families, and/or significant others) are made available when feasible. Counseling is provided by qualified professionals with an appropriate state license, if required. Additional consultation services are obtained when the need arises. Due to the high percentage of Native American juveniles in the system, reasonable provisions for visitation by the extended family, tribal elders, and tribal members are also made, provided this does not interfere with or disrupt the safe operation of the facility.

———

RESPONSE TO WRITTEN QUESTIONS SUBMITTED BY HON. TIM JOHNSON TO HON. TIMOTHY Q. PURDON

Question. As you know, jurisdictional issues can be a nightmare for both tribal and local law enforcement agencies. The Tribal Law and Order Act encourages the use of cooperative agreements. How is the DOJ providing technical assistance to tribal, local, and state agencies and what type of barriers have you witnessed in the process between agencies coming to an agreement?

Answer. The Department is working towards ensuring that both tribal and federal criminal justice systems are equipped with the authority and resources needed to ensure public safety in Indian country. To this end, the Department continues its work to strengthen relationships with federally recognized tribes, improve the coordination of training and information-sharing, and enhance tribal capacity, so that together the tribal and federal governments can provide effective law enforcement and prosecutions in Indian country.

Strengthening partnerships and tribal self-governance was a major theme of the Attorney General's message to tribal leaders on November 13, 2013, at the White House Tribal Nations Conference, where he announced a proposed statement of principles to guide the Department's work with federally recognized tribes. As the Attorney General said, ''As a result of these partnerships—and the efforts of everyone here—our nation is poised to open a new era in our government-to-government relationships with sovereign tribes.''

United States Attorneys' Offices are engaged in an unprecedented level of collaboration with tribal law enforcement, consulting regularly with them on crime-fighting strategies in each District, joining in Federal/tribal task forces, sharing case and grant information, training investigators, and cross-deputizing tribal police and prosecutors to enforce Federal law and to allow those deputized individuals to bring cases directly to Federal court. For example, the Department's enhanced Tribal Special Assistant United States Attorney (SAUSA) program is an important tool contributing to improved collaboration. Tribal SAUSAs, who are cross-deputized tribal prosecutors, are able to prosecute crimes in both tribal court and federal court as appropriate. These Tribal SAUSAs serve to strengthen a tribal government's ability to fight crime and to increase the USAO's coordination with tribal law enforcement personnel. The work of Tribal SAUSAs can also help to accelerate a tribal criminal justice system's implementation of TLOA and VAWA 2013. The Department's prioritization of Indian country crime and the increase in federal resources are indicative of our efforts to bolster the faith and confidence that tribal leaders and tribal community members have in the criminal justice system.

The COPS Office is also developing a Tribal Public Law 280 Policing Partnerships project. To strengthen the relationship between tribal law enforcement, non-tribal law enforcement, and U.S./States Attorneys in Public Law 280 sites, Strategic Applications International (SAI) will leverage its vast experience in facilitating strategy and action planning summits to address crime, drugs, and other social issues in partnership with law enforcement and key stakeholders, together with our experience in working with tribal law enforcement. The program will include approximately four sites where a two-day site specific Community Oriented Policing Training augmented with cultural dialogue training and action planning will be delivered. Participants will include Sheriffs, Chiefs of Police, U.S. Attorneys, and Tribal Leaders. The results of the onsite technical assistance will aid in the development of a web-based training curriculum tailored to Public Law 280 communities to enhance tribal and non-tribal law enforcement cooperation. The program goal is to improve public safety on tribal lands by developing a training program that builds the knowledge, skills and abilities of tribal law enforcement agencies to build more effective relationships with non-tribal law enforcement to advance community policing. This project is in its initial stages as the four on-site locations are selected and training and technical assistance begin.

The COPS Office funded the creation of a training curriculum and technical assistance effort that focuses on collaboration among tribal and local law enforcement, including the development of MOUs/MOAs/Cross-Deputization agreements that is provided by the Western Community Policing Institute. Through this program, now funded by BJA, WCPI offers regional trainings that focus on building effective and efficient collaborative law enforcement partnerships throughout Indian Country to address the unique public safety threats to tribal communities and their neighboring jurisdictions. The training curricula will include understanding cultural diversity issues, identifying stakeholders, the need for regional collaboration, and how to develop effective memorandums of understandings and agreements.

BJA also has a robust portfolio of training and technical assistance to support intergovernmental collaboration agreements. Working with the Tribal Law and Policy Institute, BJA is sponsoring state-tribal court forums and meetings to support interagency collaboration agreements, meetings and sharing of codes and resource materials. BJA also sponsors the "Walking on Common Ground" Web Site, which serves as an ongoing comprehensive resource highlighting promising practices in tribal/state court collaboration and providing resource toolkits for those wishing to replicate such practices. This site provides extensive information and resources concerning tribal/state/federal court collaboration and encourages intergovernmental collaboration and cooperation. BJA is also working with the Oregon Health and Science University to support the promotion of the joint jurisdiction court model.

DOJ's Office for Victims of Crime (OVC)'s American Indian/Alaska Native Sexual Assault Nurse Examiner-Sexual Assault Response Team Initiative (AI/AN SANE–SART) addresses the comprehensive needs of tribal victims of sexual violence, a crime that research has shown to be epidemic in many AI/AN communities and has been mired in part due to jurisdictional complexities. From the outset of the project in 2010, OVC and its federal, state, local, and tribal partners have focused on the challenge of working together to provide coordinated, communitybased, victim-centered responses to sexual violence. The 5-year project includes five components: (1) pilot testing the development and implementation of a SANE–SART response at three tribal demonstration sites in both PL 280 and non PL 280 states; (2) providing national SANE–SART coordinators for the Indian Health Service and the Federal Bureau of Investigation; (3) offering tailored training and technical assistance for tribal communities interested in developing a coordinated community response to sexual violence; (4) establishing the National Coordination Committee on the American Indian/Alaska Native Sexual Assault Nurse Examiner—Sexual Assault Response Team Initiative as a federal advisory committee for the initiative; and (5) developing a national strategy for improving the systemic response—at the tribal, state, and federal levels—to sexual assault committed against AI/AN women. To date, the National Coordination Committee has developed recommendations that focus on four major areas: (1) federal agency collaboration at the local level; (2) Department of Justice personnel policy changes; (3) Department of Justice grant solicitations and funding; and (4) public safety and public health. OVC expects that the Committee will present their recommendations to Attorney General Holder in the next 1–3 months.

The SMART Office has encouraged states to assist tribes to implement SORNA. When specific problems are noted by tribes, the SMART Office will contact the state sex offender registry representatives and facilitate communication with the tribes. At the SMART Office Workshops, sessions are specifically held to have state sex offender registry officials meet with the tribes implementing SORNA in their states. The SMART Office has also encouraged states to utilize both their Adam Walsh Act grant funds and re-allocation funds to assist tribes and/or create liaison positions to assist with tribes implementing SORNA. One state has utilized its SORNA re-allocation funds for this exact purpose to fund a liaison to the tribes. The result of such collaborations has been the expansion of criminal justice information sharing, creation of task forces for apprehending offenders, MOU's where states handle certain aspects of the registration process for tribes, and situations where tribes have used SMART grants funds to purchase hardware and software that is utilized not only by the tribes but by partner localities as well.

RESPONSE TO WRITTEN QUESTIONS SUBMITTED BY HON. MARK BEGICH TO HON. TIMOTHY Q. PURDON

Question 1. I want to ask about the Coordinated Tribal Assistance Solicitation (CTAS) grant program that you mentioned. If an Alaska Native tribe applies, and is successful in securing a CT AS grant, would the tribe be permitted to use this funding for the execution and implementation of intergovernmental agreements with the State? I would like to receive a formal response from DOJ.

Answer. Generally-speaking, CT AS grant funds could be used for costs associated with the "the execution and implementation of intergovernmental agreements" between an Alaska Native tribe and the State of Alaska, including funding legal support to assist a village/tribe in its discussions with the State. It would be advisable, however, for the village/tribe (or other entity that may be the CTAS grant recipient) to coordinate closely with the appropriate awarding agency program office regarding any such proposed use of funds in advance, to receive approval prior to incurring any expenses for legal fees for these purposes, as a number of limitations may also apply.

With respect to program authority, there may be limitations on the uses to which certain CTAS funds may be put. As an example, if the subject matter of an intergovernmental agreement funded with CT AS grant funds for corrections and corrections alternatives also covered matters unrelated to corrections/corrections alternatives, funding the full costs (as opposed to proportional costs) of legal support related to that specific agreement (with CTAS corrections funds) would generally pose legal concerns and would need to be examined closely.

In addition, cost principles and other guidance on permissible uses of federal grant award funds under applicable law (including DOJ regulations), DOJ policies, and OMB cost circulars apply to the question of hiring attorneys; these cost principles and other guidance specify both permissible and impermissible uses of federal grant award funds for legal costs and attorney's fees.

Cost-/use-of-funds considerations include the following:

- Appendix A to 2 CFR Part 225(C)(l)—To be allowable, costs must be necessary and reasonable, allocable, and not prohibited under law or excluded under award terms/conditions or other applicable rules, regulations, or policies. (For example, note that "consultant rate" costs proposed to pay attorneys or other grant-supported consultants may require prior approval.)
- Appendix B to 2 CFR Part 225(10)(b)—"Legal expenses required in the administration of Federal programs are allowable." In this case, the intergovernmental agreement being negotiated would need to be connected to the tribal administration of the specific program funded with Federal funds appropriated for that purpose.

- Appendix B to 2 CFR Part 225(32)(c)—Cost allowability of "retainer fees . . . must be supported by available or rendered evidence of bona fide services available or rendered." Records would need to be kept to document that such retainer fees are supported.
- Appendix B to 2 CFR Part 225 specifies the following impermissible uses of federal grant award funds relating to legal costs—
  - —5. Legal costs relating to "bad debts" (and debt collection);
  - —10. Legal costs for prosecution of claims against the Federal Government
- Lobbying prohibitions/disclosure requirements at 18 U.S.C. 1913 and 31 U.S.C. 1352 as implemented by 28 CFR Part 69 may also be implicated in the event that the grant funded attorneys hired by the tribe/village interact with State legislative officials in order to move discussions/negotiations regarding any proposed agreement forward, and such interaction(s) involve, as part of the agreement discussions/negotiations, a change in or adoption of any Federal, State, or local law, regulation, or policy. Without explicit statutory authority, Federal grant award funds generally may not be used for such lobbying activities.

Question 2. In your written testimony you comment that DOJ is carefully studying the recommendations in the *Roadmap* report, and that you will be reaching out to stakeholders to seek additional input. Can you provide the Committee with more details, how will you be reaching out to stakeholders, and what DOJ's timeline will be for completing outreach and submitting additional information to this Committee?

Answer. The DOJ continues to be committed to exploring the recommendations in the *Roadmap*. In dedicating an entire chapter to Alaska early on in the report, the Commission made it clear that this needs to be a specific priority for Federal agencies. In June, the Associate Attorney General visited Alaska to explore some of the issues raised in the report. This visit was meant as an information gathering trip as well as a signal to Alaska Natives of the DOJ's commitment to addressing long-standing concerns in their communities. An additional trip to Alaska by DOJ officials is expected to take place in September/October 2014. The DOJ is also in the process of fulfilling responsibilities under the Tribal Law and Order Act to consult with Alaska Natives and Alaska state representatives on continuation of the Alaska Rural Justice and Law Enforcement Commission; there will be a series of consultations on this topic which will be scheduled for early fall.

In addition to our increased efforts in Alaska, the DOJ continues to hold consultations and listening sessions and collect feedback on issues affecting DOJ activities and policies in Indian Country, including implementation of VA WA 2013, children exposed to violence, voting rights, juvenile justice, detention, reentry and approaches to funding such as CT AS. As we have worked toward better solutions to specific issues affecting American Indians and Alaska Natives, we have also developed a Statement of Principles to guide and inform all of the Department's interactions with federally recognized Indian tribes. Our Statement of Principles will memorialize our ongoing commitment to serve partners in fighting crime and enforcing the law in Indian country. Consultations on our principles have concluded, and the final version is being prepared for publication. The DOJ will continue to expand our efforts to reach out to stakeholders on these and other important issues affecting American Indians and Alaska Natives, and will be happy to continue to provide additional information on our progress to the Committee.

———

Written response to the following questions was not available at the time this hearing went to print.

WRITTEN QUESTIONS SUBMITTED BY HON. HEIDI HEITKAMP TO
HON. KEVIN WASHBURN

Question 1. Last fall, I heard a story about a teenage girl from Spirit Lake in federal detention because of substance addiction. She requested access to mental health counseling to help her deal with the reasons for her drug abuse. She also wanted to continue her education while she was detained because she was already two grades behind and was continuing to fall further back. What is the BIA doing to ensure access to counseling and educational services for incarcerated youth?

Question 2. At the Turtle Mountain Reservation in Belcourt, North Dakota, the BIA is having difficulty filling vacant positions for law enforcement officers. I understand Belcourt's remote location and lack of affordable housing contributes to recruitment issues, but this is also a common and long-standing challenge across reservation communities. What is the Department doing to fill law enforcement vacancies, particularly those in remote areas with limited housing?

Question 3. I frequently hear about the data deficit in Indian Country and how it impacts policy decisions here in Washington. The *Roadmap* found the pilot High Priority Performance Goal (HPPG) Initiative underscored the need for law enforcement to be trained to collect robust qualitative and quantitative data. What changes has the BIA instituted to address this data deficit?

Question 4. Many large land based tribes in my state and other Great Plains states are so vast in size their area is comparable to and larger than some of the small New England states. On these reservations, officers have to travel significant distances over poor roads to respond to emergency calls. Law enforcement budgets are strained by the impacts to response vehicles resulting from traveling long distances over bad roads and by fluctuations in gas prices. Additionally, many of these tribes do not have adequate facilities to house offenders locally. What steps are being taken to improve parity and provide long term base funding to ensure large land based tribes have the resources to provide timely responses to emergency calls and house offenders locally?

Question 5. I understand block grants provide a valuable tool for developing pilot projects and enhancing programs. However the *Roadmap* suggests since grant funding is not renewable, the current grant system creates inhibits long-term budget planning and has resulted in documented instances of funding shortfalls after new projects are completed. What steps are being taken to provide flexibility in grant funding for circumstances where there is inadequate base funding or for emergency funding needs?

Question 5a. What steps are being taken to ensure grant-based funding is used to build capacity and sustainability so programs may continue even after grant funding lapses?

WRITTEN QUESTIONS SUBMITTED BY HON. TIM JOHNSON TO
HON. KEVIN WASHBURN

Question 1. Mr. Washburn, many tribes face a shortage of law enforcement officers. In South Dakota, our reservations cover hundreds of miles, making it difficult for officers to travel to assist as backup or to track down leads. How will you apply what your agency has learned from the High Priority Performance Goal to other reservations, especially during this tough financial climate?

Question 2. Tribes are facing hardships when it comes to funding for detention facilities. How are you working with other agencies to address the problem of dilapidated and crowded facilities?

WRITTEN QUESTIONS SUBMITTED BY HON. MARK BEGICH TO
HON. KEVIN WASHBURN

Question 1. Are there ways that tribes/tribal courts/tribal police in Alaska can access BIA tribal justice funds, without retroceding P.L. 280 status?

Question 2. Would BIA consider changing existing restrictions that prohibit Alaska tribes from accessing BIA tribal justice funds to enhance public safety in Alaska Native villages?

Question 3. Are there other funding pools within DOI that Alaska tribes can access to enhance village public safety?

Question 4. Do you agree with the reports' findings, that Alaska tribes' ability to take land-into-trust will enhance village public safety?

Question 5. Do you support amending the definition of "Indian Country" to clarify that Native allotments and Native-owned town sites in Alaska as Indian Country?